Careers in Sociology

Third Edition

W. Richard Stephens, Jr.
Eastern Nazarene College

Boston   New York   San Francisco
Mexico City   Montreal   Toronto   London   Madrid   Munich   Paris
Hong Kong   Singapore   Tokyo   Cape Town   Sydney

This book is dedicated to:
Deb, Ashlee and Billy

ISBN 0-205-37922-2

Printed in the United States of America

10 9 8 7 6 5 4 3 2   08 07 06 05

CAREERS IN SOCIOLOGY
Yes, You Can Get a Job with a Degree in Sociology!

TABLE OF CONTENTS

PREFACE

The genesis of this book is the classroom and ultimately the interests of students in those classrooms. Most students take their first course in sociology because it is required by some general education or major curriculum. My experience at a small liberal arts college bears this out. Yet, out of 800 students we have approximately 60 majors. The vast majority of these students decide on sociology only after having been required to take a course such as Principles of Sociology, Social Problems, or Marriage and Family. The point is, the content of sociology is interesting, and most students will find something that piques their interest in the courses. But what happens next catches many teachers off guard. The interested student will comment and ask, "I find topics interesting, but is there anything I can do if I were to major in sociology?"

All too often a meaningful answer is not forthcoming. By this I mean that an eighteen- or nineteen-year-old student is interested in knowing what kind of employment he/she can expect, including information on income. The answers typically offered are rarely so specific. Instead, students are told there are some general areas where non-academic sociology could be practiced (such as social policy), but with little or no direction as to how to approach that field as a career. The difficulty is matching the content interest of a teacher with the career implication interests of students. To this end I began, several years ago, collecting material on graduates from my department and from colleagues in non-academic employment across the country. Compiled into what I call character profiles, these document careers in ways meaningful to the questions students have been asking. The result is that sociology becomes more than interesting, it becomes relevant.

This last statement is particularly challenging to those already established in the discipline. Relevance to the population of professors is obvious. I often tell my students that I cannot help but to see life from a sociological perspective. I even observe myself and my family this way, as I did during a recent six-month visiting professorship in Russia. But such an orientation cannot be expected of students who are in my class simply because they are required to be there. And when the inevitable questions come, relevance must be established, not assumed.

In the following pages student and teacher alike will come face-to-face with a sociology which goes beyond interest to impact. Character Profiles (CP) will document the work and careers of persons who chose to pursue a degree in sociology. The CP's illustrate some of the variety of career paths people have followed with degrees in sociology. Each CP will be comprised of information detailing specifics about the work or career, sociological aspects of the work itself, degree preparation and requirements for employment, information on how the job was acquired, salary, and future prospects. In short, each CP actually answers in a specific case,

"What can I <u>do</u> with a degree in sociology?"

Finally, in an appendix, "A Workbook for Job Seekers in Sociology" is provided, as a special contribution by the Society for Applied Sociology. Here, students are led through a rationally organized and sequential career development program. As a workbook students are encouraged to actively fill in the spaces provided for implementing such concepts as vision statements, networking, mentoring, etc. The point is, it is not too early to begin the process of job seeking and career development. It takes time. Whether a student stays in sociology is not the point. Making thoughtful choices is the point.

As stated at the beginning, the genesis of this book is a most challenging question offered by students -- "What can be done with this degree?" Therefore, this book is targeted at students, rather than teachers or professors. It is a challenge to students to take a requirement and turn it into an advantage, to move from interest to application, and to invest in the idea of a career, any career, through a discipline this book demonstrates to be most relevant, sociology.

ACKNOWLEDGMENTS

Any book, even a small one like this, is a community project. Required are many others--colleagues such as Stephen Steele, who tirelessly promotes the contributions of sociology as a discipline, and whose enthusiasm for this book provided needed motivation; Karen Hanson, Senior Editor for Sociology at Allyn and Bacon, who recognized the need for an answer to the questions of students and their parents, and who was always encouraging and supportive; The Society for Applied Sociology for the special contribution of the "Workbook"; W. Richard Stephens, Sr., my father, who can somehow offer sound and critical advice without stepping on your dreams; CP subjects who willingly told me great personal stories because they believed in the idea of this book; Harriet Colville, who read and provided meaningful editing; and my family, who provided inspiration, support, and great amounts of patience as I worked through this project.

1.

THE "INTRO" EXPERIENCE
Making the Most of your First Class in Sociology

Step #1: "Why am I in Sociology Anyway?"

If you are like most students, sociology is a new and somewhat strange discipline to be studying. It is new, in that few students entering college have even heard of it, and even fewer intend to major in it. It is strange, in that there is virtually no topic which sociology does not touch, and therefore it is difficult to see where the discipline is distinct from others. It is probably also the case that you are reading this book, and therefore taking this course, because the degree you are interested in requires it. Or, it is part of the general education requirements for all students at your college. In other words, you <u>have</u> to take this course. Have you wondered why?

The answer lies in the fact that sociology is such a topically broad discipline. If there is a central focus it is the issues, problems, trials, and triumphs of people trying to get along with each other; in other words, human relationships.

So, the discipline has something to say to people trying to get along in a structure called a family, or members of a team, or neighbors, or employees trying to figure out work relations. The point is, sociology is relevant wherever human relations are at work. It follows then, that an improved understanding of human relations should translate into better conduct of those relations. There are exceptions, of course, such as the manipulation of those relations for the benefit of some while at the expense of others. But the general point remains, sociology provides insights which are applicable to a wide array of human circumstances.

I was one of those students who took an introductory sociology class because it was required. I had all the same questions you probably now have; especially why I had to take it. Since I am now a professor of sociology then I personally have come to some satisfactory answers as to the validity and importance of the discipline. But what about others? What about you? While I have not done extensive statistical research on the matter I do have seventeen years of college-level teaching experience, including an introductory class or two in each of those years. In that time I have made some observations which I do believe can be generalized to most students. Over the course of a semester, most students will have one or both of the following experiences.

The first experience is that you will identify personally with one of

1.

more of the topics explored. You will see clearly what the discipline has to say about some aspect of human relations because you have actually experienced the phenomenon in question. For example, Emile Durkheim used the term anomie to describe the effects of radical social change on people. He was writing about the effects of mass migration from the countryside to the city in early 20th century France. On the surface, such ideas seem remote, but in class they become real as the concept is applied to our own experiences. In the case of students, nearly all experience some degree of anomie when they first encounter college or, for that matter, when they are "clueless" as to the reason they have to take sociology! The point is, the sociological concept does apply to your life. On a more topical level, you have experienced sociologically relevant phenomena such as family, socialization, peer pressure, intergenerational relations, being hired and/or fired, death, crime and deviance, religion, commercials, prejudice, etc., etc., etc. Only if you have not experienced such phenomena is sociology irrelevant to you.

The second experience is that most students will take a genuine interest in at least one of the topics covered. It could be the role of women in big business, the changing demographic face of America, the impact of new technologies on work, family life, and leisure, or issues such as universal health care and social security for the aged. Related to this last point, my introductory students participate in a one-hour-a-week elder visitation program. In this program students are paired with senior citizens from all over town and they simply visit. Most students groan, excessively, about this assignment prior to engaging in it. However, most report that the experience was a valuable one by the time the semester is completed. Often, students continue visiting their new friend after the course is completed. They found that something they had not really considered, intergenerational relations, really was interesting. The point here is, you will most likely find something interesting to the point that study of it is no longer a chore, but becomes an aspect of study and life you actually like or enjoy.

Now, take the two experiences, coming across something you have personally experienced and discovering something of special interest, and combine them. The result, while not necessarily an epiphany (if you don't know what this means, look it up!), it is nonetheless potentially significant. Your level of interest in sociology, or at least some topic within the field, has been raised. Evidence of this comes from friends and often family who notice a difference in the way their friend or child (you) now sees and talks about the world. Some will say that now you use "big" words! This will most likely happen to you. As this happens you then begin to raise questions about yourself and your place in the scheme of things. This is natural, it is to be expected, and it is a indicator of maturity. You are becoming more conscious of what is happening to and around you.

You are now in a position to be an active participant in your and other people's lives, rather than being primarily acted upon by others. We call this, empowerment.

Step #2: "OK, I'm Interested, but is There a Future for Me in Sociology?"

It is the <u>extremely</u> rare student who comes out of high school with their mind made up to study sociology in college. The number is something like 3 out of every 10,000 (Howery, 1985). Yikes! If it were not for the requirements most colleges impose on students you would find a lot of academic sociologists roaming the streets. But somehow, at a college like mine we have nearly 60 majors out of a student body of 800. Since they do not typically come in as freshmen with sociology "on the brain" then it is the case that they are "converted" after some introductory encounter. For example, I took a group of ten or so students to Russia for a month to study the transformations occurring there. The study tour satisfied the sociology requirement for general education. Most students said it would be an interesting way of "getting sociology out of the way." Not much respect for the discipline in that statement. Regardless, the trip, and sociological lessons learned, influenced at least two students to choose sociology as their primary or secondary major.

What I am suggesting is, it could happen to you; you could choose to major in sociology. It has happened to others. The question is, how should you respond? What type of questions should you ask? How does one go about pursuing sociology as a major? Is there a future in sociology? This choice, making sociology your major, or part of a double major, is a critical choice, and should not be made lightly. Unfortunately, too many professors of sociology are not well-equipped to help you with this choice. What follows are some considerations which should be a part of any decision you make.

Typically, a student will stop by after class someday and ask, "Do you have a handout or something that will tell me what types of jobs I can get if I were to major in sociology?" For some professors this is a most uncomfortable question. I know, I have been questioned like this and in the past I have been unable to meaningfully answer. Yes, graduate school and a career in teaching is a valid option; but it is not a sufficient option. There simply is not enough room in the teaching profession to absorb all who pursue a degree in sociology. Besides, not every one is ready to commit another four to ten years to their studies. The real point, however, is that if the student was interested in an academic career they would have asked "How do I become a professor?" not, "Are there jobs I could get if I majored in sociology?"

So, back to the typical student. What I usually do is have the student make an appointment so that we can talk about the options, academic and nonacademic, those requiring graduate school and those not, etc. I also try to find out what topical interests the student has so that I can then be more precise in my advice. However, there is little material available which straightforwardly answers our typical student's questions. To compensate, I make arrangements for my students to meet with former sociology students who have "real" jobs; i.e., non-academic jobs. This book is a step in the direction of putting in your hands that straightforward answer. Interestingly, often when students ask about majoring in sociology many go ahead and take steps to declare sociology as a first or second major. This is where a more interesting and very important phenomenon occurs. Mom and Dad get into the act.

In my experience, once the typical student decides on sociology there develops a sense of energy and anticipation about the future. But the future is as much on the collective minds of parents as it is on the mind of the son or daughter. At some point the student tells Mom and Dad what their interests are and what their decision is. And, Mom and Dad do what good parents should do; they test the decision. Recently I had lunch with a parent of junior sociology major who is interested in a career in criminal justice. This parent and I have had several in-depth discussions about his son. At one point the father said, "The bottom line is, will my son be able to get a job when he graduates? By that time we will have spent $60,000 on his education. That's quite an investment. We want to make sure he has a future." Such sentiment is valid and is to be expected. Unfortunately, in my opinion, it is a sentiment not often recognized by my colleagues. If not handled well, a student's dreams can be lost. Therefore, this book is as much for parents as it is for students. In fact, I advise you to share this with anyone who is interested in and concerned about your future.

Now, back to the question regarding the future. The short answer is, yes, there is a future. And it is a future which is bright and growing brighter as time passes. It is bright because people with vision have begun to take the central and universal ideas of sociology and have begun looking for ways to put them into action. This effort in itself is neither new nor unique. Many other disciplines have been doing this for decades or centuries. Some have been doing this for years, but with tools and concepts derived from sociology. Marketing experts, political pollsters, etc. have been employing basic survey research techniques and statistical procedures developed over time in sociology for very practical purposes. It is also the case that sociology has developed and given birth to whole new disciplines such as criminal justice/criminology, gerontology, women's studies, black studies, demography, and social work. Each of these has put the discipline to work in very specific ways. Now, sociology as a discipline, and sociologists as a profession, are asserting their collective strengths. And, we find that more and more these strengths are finding expression and applications outside the classroom. For example, 95% of the graduates from my department work in non-academic settings. But what are the broader trends. Consider the following.

In 1988, the U.S. Office of Personal Management established a position - classification standard for sociology. This means that the federal government officially recognizes the specific contributions which sociology can make. The standard for "Sociology GS-184" begins with the following statement:

> This series includes positions which involve professional work requiring a knowledge of sociology and sociological methods specifically related to the establishment, validation, interpretation, and application of knowledge about social processes. Sociologists study specialized areas such as: changes in the character, size, distribution, and composition of the population: social mechanisms for enforcing compliance with widely accepted norms and for controlling deviance; social phenomena having to do with human health and disease; the structure and operation of organizations; and the complex interrelationship of the individual and society.
>
> Sociologists are concerned primarily with the study of patterns of group and organizational behavior, social interaction, and social situations in which interaction occurs. The emphasis is on the patterns of behavior that are characteristic of social groups, organizations, institutions, and nations. Some sociologists perform sociological research, others apply sociological principles and findings, and some perform a combination of both kinds of work.

Based on this standard, five specializations are recommended, including demography, law and social control, medical sociology, organizational analysis, and social psychology.

In addition, the standard advises prospective applicants that sociology is appropriate education for work in other areas such as but not limited to:

GS-020 Community Planning Series
GS-101 Social Work Series
GS-131 International Relations Series
GS-135 Foreign Agricultural Affairs Series
GS-140 Manpower Research and Analysis Series
GS-142 Manpower Development Series
GS-160 Civil Rights Analysis Series
GS-185 Social Work Series
GS-230 Employee Relations Series
GS-685 Public Health Program Specialist Series
GS-696 Consumer Safety Series
GS-1150 Industrial Specialist Series

The prospects have further brightened to the point where over the last ten years new associations of sociologists who work primarily in non-academic settings have been established and are flourishing. These would include organizations such as:

The Society for Applied Sociology
The Sociological Practice Association
The Chicago Sociological Practice Association
The District of Columbia Sociological Society
The Sociologists in Business
The Sociological Practice Section of the American Sociological Association

What follows is a partial listing of non-academic settings where sociologists are currently employed, compiled from the directories of the associations just referenced (Stephens, 1994):

Where Sociological Practitioners Work

A.C. Neilsen
AT&T
Argone National Laboratory
Army Research Institute
American Bar Association
American International Group
American Medical Association
American Express
Atari
Avon Products Inc.
Boys Town Center

Litigation Sciences, Inc.
Mayatech Corporation
NASA
National Analysts
National Institutes of Health
NBC
New York Business Group on Health
New York City Fire Department
CBS, Inc.
Citibank, N.A.

City of Chicago Department of Housing
Cleveland Clinic
Equitable Life Federation of
    Protestant Churches
Financial News Network
G.S. Searle Laboratories
General Accounting Office
General Electric
General Foods
General Motors Research Laboratories
Hughes Aircraft Co.
Hutchings Psychiatric Center
Illinois Criminal Justice Authority
Internal Revenue Service
KMPG Peat Marwick
New York City Human Resources
    Administration
Rand Corporation
Rockefeller Foundation

Rubbermaid Inc.
Saint Vicents Hospital
Sears, Roebuck, & Co.
Standard and Poor
The Equitable
The Gallup Organization
The Public Health Foundation
The Vanderveer Group
U.S. Bureau of the Census
U.S. Department of Agriculture
U.S. Department of Energy
U.S. Department of Health
    and Human Services
Wells Fargo Bank
Young & Rubican
Xerox

As you can see, there is great variety to the job settings. There is similar variety to non-academic job titles, as evidenced by the GS-184 series standard. But how do you translate the potential of a discipline like sociology into an actual career? The parent with the $60,000 invested in his son appreciates potential, but how can his son go from degree to job? Does one just look for "sociologist wanted" job ads? Is graduate school necessary? Even if a job is available and you take it, can you make a living? These are reasonable and important questions, and the remainder of this book is dedicated to answering them.

Step #3: "What Will I Achieve by Reading This Book?"

By now you should have noticed something about this book which is different from most other academic texts. While I am professor of sociology, I have not written this book for my colleagues, other sociologists. Therefore, it is not full of "sociologese" -- big sociological words and complex sentences. It is written in a much more familiar style. It is as if we are having a conversation about sociology and your future. Obviously, you cannot talk back, but I have tried to anticipate some of your comments and questions so as to maintain the sense of conversation. You do not need a lecture on your future, you need advice and perspective. Therefore, if you stay in a conversational mode this book will make more sense. What I mean is that this book will not merely present information for you to swallow and then "cough" back up on a test. That approach simply will not be satisfactory when discussing your future. You must actively

7.

participate in pursuing your own future, and I believe this book can be used as a jumping-off point.

The pages to follow are composed into what I call, "character profiles" (CP for short). Each CP is a brief overview of the career choices and activities of some real person who has at least one degree in sociology. While the person is real, names and other identifying details have been altered to insure anonymity. Anonymity is important, not because these people have something to hide, but because they have been willing to provide a lot of personal detail, including items like income. The CP will walk you, the student, through the professional lives of each subject. Included will be information about degrees earned, explanations for interest in sociology, job history, career development, and income. Special mention will be made regarding how these people see their degree(s) in sociology as it relates to their careers. Advice is also given to students who are considering their own post-graduate lives. Now, not all CP's follow exactly the same format. But then, neither do our lives. Do rest assured however, that all CP's are based on real people, all of whom are currently practicing sociology in some context.

Just above I mentioned your participation as you work through this book. Remember, this book is not so much about sociology as it is about people who make their living and careers with sociology. As you read, write questions and/or comments about career development in the margins. Don't just highlight or you will end up with whole pages highlighted! Think about the choices these people made. What kinds of skills do they have? What values and ideas do they promote? How did they get their jobs? What advice do they have, both explicit and implied? If you were to create a typical career development model from among all the CP's, what is the common ground? In addition, can you find connections between the CP's and some ideas or material from the main text for your course? At the end of each CP, some related text chapters are suggested. You see, it is my hope that the CP's will serve as models for your own choices. It matters not whether you are seriously considering sociology as a major. The CP's contain lessons that transcend disciplines. In fact, many of the people, in my opinion, have transcended traditional conceptions of sociology. The goal is not to make you into a professional sociologist per se. It is to pass on to you significant skills and perspectives, and a legacy which makes you a thoughtful, and therefore an empowered person.

The CP's are not arranged in any particular order, nor do they cover all combinations and permutations of sociological study and career. As mentioned, they are brief. So, it is possible for you to pick this book up, read a CP making comments and asking questions, and put it down in fifteen to twenty minutes. Further, because each CP is self-contained, you can read this book in any order. The effort is to present a book which is interesting, helpful, and user-friendly.

Also, take a look, now, at the appendix of this book. Here you will find "A Workbook for Job Seekers in Sociology." The workbook, contributed by the Society for Applied Sociology, provides a step-by-step plan of action for pursuing a job as well as developing a career. These things, jobs and careers, do not just happen, they are produced by your actions and choices in some context of opportunities. Either you are ready and prepared to make decisions which could influence the next forty to fifty years of your life, or you are not. The workbook is a step in the right direction.

One last piece of advice before you proceed. Whatever career dreams you have, consider the following. Your work options can be divided broadly into two categories, or worlds. One is the world of people. The other is the world of things. Now examine your interests and your dreams. Do you see these as focused primarily on people, or is your focus primarily on technical matters, things. My brother used to say that he was going into medicine so that he could deal with concrete issues, exact answers. He could not stand the ambiguity of any of the other "philosophies." Now he has been a practicing rural family physician for nearly 10 years. When asked about concrete issues he admits that nearly all of what he does is a matter of judgment. His position in the community and his reputation are as much a part of his profession as knowing how to delivery babies. The point is, you must think hard and creatively to come up with a career that does not bring you into close contact with others. The argument could be made that, on this basis, there is no career that cannot be profited by a sociological perspective. This is not to say that sociology should, therefore, be your degree of choice. But it does suggest that there is a significant contribution sociology can make to any career. Think about this as you read about people already in careers, because in doing so you are thinking about your future and your career.

2.

SOCIOLOGY AND CAREERS
IN INTERNATIONAL RELATIONS

Sarah Johnson works as a Branch Chief for the International Research Division (IRD) of the United States' Department of Foreign Relations. James Richards also works for the IRD as a research analyst within the office of research. While different in detail, both Sarah and James have had education and career paths which have developed as a result of sensing and seizing opportunities. Neither of them suspected while in school that they would end up at IRD. IRD is a federal government agency charged with responsibility for producing and distributing data related to international relations. Among other things this agency oversees and produces public opinion survey research conducted in foreign countries. One purpose of these surveys is to provide information for U.S. foreign policy formation. Other responsibilities include administering foreign exchange programs, the development of traveling exhibits to communicate information about the U.S., and responsibility for programming such as Voice of America (radio programs broadcast from the United states to many parts of the world).

James' education and career path did not begin with sociology. His B.A. was in history, but did include some courses in sociology. Most importantly, James studied the Russian language. After graduation he began a master's degree in an interdisciplinary Soviet Studies program. Here he was able to combine his growing interest in Russian language with a study of Soviet/Russian society. Sociology, both as a point of view and as a method of data collection and analysis, was an essential ingredient in constructing an adequate and accurate picture of Soviet life. The importance of this kind of study is best understood in light of the ongoing "Cold War" at that time. The simple fact is, any country's present and future is inextricably bound to the present and future of Russia. Therefore, it is imperative that one have a full understanding of Russian society.

After receiving his M.A., James decided to stay in graduate school and pursue the Ph.D. In this endeavor he built upon his foundation in Russian studies but decided to pursue his degree in sociology. For James, the tools of sociology and the perspective of the sociologist were especially relevant to producing good information about America's "Cold War" enemy. In combination, James' ability to read and speak Russian and his skills in sociological methods and analysis produced an opportunity for travel and study in the Soviet Union. With funding from the International

Research and Exchange board James conducted research on patterns of educational attainment in the USSR. Unique to this research was the need to somehow get around Soviet censors who were monitoring his work. Eventually, James was able to access the dissertations of Russian scholars as a means of assessing educational attainment. According to James, this was the only way around the information restriction imposed by the censors.

After completion of the Ph.D., James spent about six years in teaching and post-doctoral research. During this time, he made several research visits to Washington, D.C. While there, he made it a point to make a number of contacts, thus expanding his personal network. His dream was to find a way to pursue his interests in Soviet Russia and employ his skills as a sociologist. One of his contacts had been with IRD, and in the early 1980's U.S.-Soviet relations were deteriorating. The U.S. and the U.S.S.R. were engaged in a sizable arms build-up. There was unrest in the U.S. and growing concern about nuclear holocaust. The movie "The Day After" was one of the most watched television programs of all time. The Star Wars defense plan was proposed and research on it begun. It was a time when "good" information was absolutely necessary. Policy was being formed which could shape our future for generations to come. In this environment James Richards began working for IRD as a research analyst.

Sarah Johnson's path to IRD was quite different. Her education was much more focused on sociology as her B.A., M.A. and Ph.D. were all earned in sociology. After receiving her M.A., Sarah took a job as a junior researcher for a public school district which was attempting to implement court-ordered desegregation. Her particular expertise was research methods and statistics, and she had a lot of experience with computers. The project was to evaluate the impact of desegregation, by focusing on student achievement, particularly the achievement of minorities. For this it became evident that she needed additional skills in statistics and methods and therefore began taking advanced course work in these areas. The research project required the employment of multiple methods of data collection, from survey questionnaires to document searches, to direct observations of children in buses as angry protestors threw stones. Sarah was getting a very up-close look at the need for, potential, and difficulty of research on domestic policy issues.

After the desegregation project, Sarah returned to her special interest in medicine, and taught in a medical school. Courses there included medical ethics, history of medicine, and medical research. She also conducted medical research and involved medical students in research methods. According to Sarah, it is important that the medical community see the delivery of medical services as much more than biological variables. Included are social structure, economics, the organization of health care delivery systems, etc.

After teaching in medical school Sarah next followed a long-standing interest in foreign travel and went to Europe. While there, she made contact with Radio Free Europe and Radio Liberty. Here, her degree

11.

background in sociology, particularly methods, opened many doors. At this time the Cold War was still driving a wedge between Eastern and Western Europe, as well as between the USSR and the U.S. Because of this, it was important to try to understand how people in Eastern Europe perceived the situation, themselves, the West, the future generally and prospects for peace. Through the sponsorship of western radio programming, a series of surveys was commissioned. The task was to "get a handle" on Eastern Europe at the grass-roots level. The problem was that grass-roots research was simply not possible prior to the tearing down of the Berlin Wall. So, a research program was put together which sought to interview Eastern Europeans traveling to Western Europe for business or pleasure. To accomplish this, Eastern European immigrants to the West were hired to meet Eastern European visitors as they arrived in places like Vienna, Paris, etc. The immigrants would then offer to serve the travelers as hosts to the city and show them around, interpret, help them shop, find lodging, etc. These interactions provided the needed opportunity to discuss specific issues. In this way, the project sought to get at the grass-roots level of perception and public opinion in the closed society of Eastern Europe. Sarah credits her sociological discipline for opening doors to this kind of research opportunity, and for providing within her a flexibility and adaptability to create productive research designs.

After several years, Sarah returned to the U.S. to look for new challenges. While in Washington, D.C., she became aware that the IRD was in need of experienced researchers for Eastern Europe. In particular, there was focus on Eastern European media and how study of it can be revealing of a society's inner workings, and the values and perceptions of its people. Her decision was to accept a position as a Branch Chief within IRD, managing a team of social scientists as they research a variety of foreign policy related issues.

Now, at IRD, James Richards and Sarah are colleagues who focus their education, skills, and experience on research designed to increase our understanding of formerly closed societies in the former Soviet Union and Eastern Europe. Public opinion research is the primary focus, although other emphases focus on the role of media in these societies. For example, newspapers and radio and television broadcasts are monitored, and content analyses are conducted so as to determine the slant and directions of public information. The public opinion surveys directly question average people regarding their opinions of foreign countries (in particular the U.S.), what they believe is problematic about our international relations, what do they think about new political and economic structures, do they understand democratic electoral processes, etc.

It is Sarah's job, as Branch Chief, to oversee the work of agency researchers as they study Eastern Europe. This means that she works on setting research agendas, including where and what will be studied. She assigns work to researchers with various specialties. And, she must "stay on top" of the research process in order to insure task completion as well as the integrity of the data. In a real sense, Sarah is managing other social scientists which she says, "can be quite a challenge." The work requires a lot of skill and creativity which does not lend itself well to strict work guidelines. Most difficult, she says, is "boiling information down to one paragraph or one page." She needs to be able to pass on meaningful information in the most efficient manner. Reports often find their way to the State Department, and even the White House. There is simply no time to read a richly detailed fifty-page report. Therefore, clear and concise writing skills are absolutely important. Thus, Sarah is responsible for overseeing research projects from their inception to their culmination.

James is involved in the actual details of doing public opinion surveys. He must match the issues with a methodology of data collection. This means, among other things, questionnaire construction. However, it also means more than a mere technical exercise. James must be sensitive to local populations, cultures, issues and interests. Toward this end, James often travels to the countries where such work is being carried out. His Russian language capabilities are most helpful in this regard. Further, he negotiates with local research firms who are in the best position to actually carry out the data collection. Here James is combining cross-cultural capabilities with basic sociological skills in order to produce the desired data. Upon completion of this phase of the research, James must then begin statistical and analytical processing of the data. In other words, he must determine what the real findings of the public opinion surveys are and what they mean.

In the work of both James and Sarah there is great dependence upon traditional sociological skills and insights. The skills focus on research methods, statistics, and writing. The insights help in understanding issues and research results with implications for policy. In addition, there is a special need for flexibility and creativity. If you cannot get information one way then you must design some other way. You must continuously access your personal networks in order to achieve your objective. You need an understanding of the interplay of macro-trends and micro-experiences. For all of these, according to both James and Sarah, sociology is "excellent preparation."

As their careers have progressed, James and Sarah have evidenced a common experience without sharing all the same details. One came to sociology late in his academic career, the other has been a sociologist from the start. One has worked primarily in one or two organizational settings, while the other has been in many different settings. While one had a deep and long-term academic interest in Eastern Europe, the other became interested only after several other interests had been pursued. The point is, James and Sarah have come to be colleagues by circuitous rather than direct routes. When asked about this and its implication for undergraduate students thinking about their careers, James offered the following advice: "Follow your interests, meet interesting people, and see what happens." Sarah advises, "You need to be ready to take advantage of opportunities when they are presented." The further point is, neither James or Sarah specifically intended to end up at IRD. But what they did intend was to seek and seize opportunities.

This ability to scope out opportunities and be flexible enough to take advantage of them has produced not only interesting career paths, but also a comfortable standard of living. James now earns in the $55,000 to $59,000 annual salary range. Entry-level researchers, depending on degrees and experience can expect salaries from the mid-$20,000's to the low $30,000's. Sarah's experience is more varied and so is her income history. While working on the desegregation project, she earned in the low to mid-$30,000's (this was over ten years ago). Her work in Europe earned $100,000 plus. Now her salary is in the mid-$60,000's. To achieve James and Sarah's level of work responsibility and income requires preparation, especially education. In their cases, sociology has certainly advanced their personal experiences and professional careers.

NOTE:

For more information important to this career see the following chapters in Sociology: A Down to Earth Approach, by James M. Henslin:

        Chapter 2 Culture
        Chapter 5 How Sociologists Do Research
        Chapter 9 Stratification in Global Perspective
        Chapter 15 Politics: Power and Authority
        Chapter 22 Social Change, Technology and the Environment

3.

SOCIOLOGY AND CAREERS
IN HEALTH CARE

Bill Lange's early contacts with undergraduate sociology were not particularly impressive. Bill was even unsure, at least early on, just what sociology was. Nonetheless, the classes he took held his interest. The issues addressed were wide-ranging and the interpretations of society began to have some meaning for him. He was especially intrigued by computer applications, research methods, and statistics. He therefore decided to complete his B.A. in sociology and pursue an M A as well. Bill admits, however, that while he was reasonably certain about his education he was not too sure about his post-graduate options. Even more, according to Bill, "My in-laws were not so sure that a degree in sociology was such a good thing for their daughter!"

In his studies Bill had focused his attention on statistical applications and had worked on several projects within the department of sociology. In fact, his experience with research while still in college proved most valuable in his later job search. In addition, Bill became aware of the real need for intelligent national data collection and analyses in a wide array of contexts. In other words, Bill found that the unique skills of the sociologist really are in wide demand, and that there are many professional opportunities if one is properly prepared.

Ultimately Bill answered an advertisement for a "research position" with the Veterans Administration. One of the primary issues within health care is cost control. How much does health care cost and what does it really produce? The research position Bill applied for required statistical and computer skills for application and analysis of a major study on cancer patient follow-up care. The medical condition being researched was lung cancer, and other studies would soon be targeting colon-rectal cancer and esophageal cancer. In all cases the patients had either surgery or chemo-therapy or both, to the point that the cancer had at least been contained. After such procedures/treatments, there is then a protocol for follow-up care. From the research the federal government wanted to find out if different kinds of follow-up care would be productive of different rates of patient survival. Specifically, should a patient who had been treated for lung cancer be required to submit to a CAT scan every six months, in order to detect new cancerous developments, or would a CAT scan every three years be sufficient to ensure the same survival rates? Or, should patients simply have an office visit with a doctor every six months and have a CAT scan only if the doctor believes one is indicated?

On the surface of the issue it would seem that being checked every six months would result in greater patient survival than being checked every three years. But as those acquainted with research have discovered, there is often a significant difference between how things seem to be, and what the facts really are. In fact, according to Bill, "Our findings so far indicate no significant difference." Now, you must understand that the federal government has paid approximately $200,000-$300,000 to have this research done. With a finding of "no significant difference" this study may seem to some as a waste of time and money. However, as Bill suggested, his sociological perspective prepares him to see the "larger picture." In this case the larger picture could work out in the following way.

A typical CAT scan costs approximately $1000; $750 for the procedure and $250 for reading or interpreting the results. For one lung cancer patient with a survival rate of 10 years, follow-up care programs of six months to three years would produce the following cost differences. CAT scans every six months for ten years would cost a minimum of $20,000 (20 visits times $1,000 per visit). CAT scans every three years would cost $3,333 (3.3 visits times $1,000 per visit). In other words, for follow-up care programs which produce essentially the same results one program is 600% to 700% more expensive than the other. Now consider the implications of these differences on a larger scale. Let's say you have 1000 lung cancer patients in need of follow-up care over a ten-year period. If your follow-up care program called for CAT scans every six months then the total cost would be approximately $20 million. However, with CAT scans conducted every three years the cost drops to $3.3 million; a difference of $16.7 million. Such a difference is pretty astonishing, but as with all findings further analysis must be done in order to fully understand the implications.

If you are a lung cancer survivor you, of course, are not interested in aggregate data. You are interested in good health. Therefore, health care decisions on the individual level are never so black and white. What does seem evident is that the quality of the relationship between the patient and his/her primary care doctor is significant to good health and post-cancer survival. So, rather than automatic CAT scans, more frequent primary care exams could substitute. And an exam protocol would indicate when CAT scans would be warranted. Obviously this means that responsibility for ordering CAT scans falls to the primary care doctor. Yet, paradoxically, it has been primary care physicians who have pushed for more frequent special exams and procedures, such as CAT scans. The reason for this is that primary care physicians have been the target of an increasing number of malpractice lawsuits. As this line of reasoning is followed then we find that the significance extends even to medical law, the rights of patients and the responsibilities of practitioners.

Bill's contributions to this research are several, all of which are based in sociological methods and theory. As the only sociologist on the research team Bill is able to bring a societal or social structural perspective to bear on issues as varied as contextualizing the research problem to evaluating data collection tools, such as surveys, for reliability and validity. As the only staff sociologist Bill finds that others within the VA search him out for advice. According to Bill, "Some doctors once came to me with a survey they had constructed to assess some aspect of their work. As with most non-sociologists the technical aspects of a survey are simply beyond them. Asking a meaningful question is more difficult than they often think. Further, how do they know if the questions they ask are at all related to the issue they are interested in?"

In addition to this Bill has primary responsibility for data management, including statistical manipulations using SPSS (Statistical Package for the Social Sciences). Here his background in methods and statistics has been most valuable. According to Bill, "My entree to this work was based more on my sociological skills in research rather than my ability to sociologically conceptualize. But now I feel as though I am able to begin introducing the kinds of questions and conceptualizations which can influence future research."

In terms of his future Bill says that he "looks forward to the next grant." His work, while within the context of the VA, is not routine or repetitious. It is project driven. In future projects Bill expects to be participating more at the front-end of the research, the proposal and grant-writing stage. Here is where he feels his more uniquely sociological perspective will have a real impact. His work is not with other sociologists, it is interdisciplinary; and that makes the work quite challenging. It is the opportunity to do medical sociology, and thereby influence the delivery of health care for good that gives Bill a real sense of satisfaction. "If we believe that sociology really is applicable to a broad array of problems then we must be in those contexts where we can put that perceived contribution to the test." Toward this end, Bill's next project is to pursue a multi-million dollar grant for research into the way anesthesia is used and delivered to patients. This long-term study has, according to Bill, "real implications for health care delivery. Further, it is an exciting project."

For those considering sociology as a major Bill advises that, "there is life after school." Special attention should be given to the basic skills and insights, such as research methods and statistics. Given that research findings are not self-evident, it is imperative that writing and speaking skills be cultivated. "If possible, do an internship or practicum. These are great ways to see just how sociology can contribute."

Finally, Bill wants it understood that he has answered his in-laws' worries. His annual income ranges in the low $20,000's for thirty hours of work per week, for now. He fully expects that to increase, though for now the work, both schedule and content, suits him just fine.

NOTE:

For more information important to this career see the following chapters in
Sociology: A Down to Earth Approach, by James M. Henslin:
        Chapter 5 How Sociologists Do Research
        Chapter 19 Medicine: Health and Illness

4.

SOCIOLOGY AND CAREERS
IN BUSINESS CONSULTATION

Janique Cordier brings to her work a wealth of experience and education. She personally embodies the concept of diversity. From French universities Janique earned her undergraduate degree in biochemistry and a master's degree in marketing. With these degrees Janique worked as a manager of a manufacturing company which produced large earth-moving equipment. As a part of her work she developed markets, and sought ways to adapt the product of the company to the needs of clients and customers. Through these activities Janique came into contact with people from a wide array of cultural backgrounds. And, she began developing a capability for cross-cultural relations.

Another part of Janique's work has been travel. Over the years she has worked as a teacher in Africa and Chile, performed market research in Japan, and finally, started her own business and lived in the United States. In addition to French she also speaks Spanish and English. As can be seen, there are many parts to Janique's life which have prepared her to be flexible and adaptive.

It was after moving to the United States that Janique began her studies in sociology. Initially, for Janique, "Sociology was a way of learning about the United States. I knew I needed to understand American culture." The discipline also provided three additional benefits. First, "It provided a unique perspective on organizational behavior." Janique came to see work and organization from a social rather than technical or strictly business perspective. For example, the sociological perspective clearly differentiates productive work from mere activity. She observed that, "Many managers are caught in the `activity trap' believing that activity equals productivity." It was the nature of work and organization that became Janique's Ph.D. emphasis.

The second benefit of sociology was the development of an array of special skills. These are primarily methodological and include abilities such as survey construction and administration, interviewing, statistical manipulation and interpretation.

The third benefit is really a skill, but is not traditionally referred to as a methodology. This benefit, this skill Janique refers to, is sensitivity to cultures and the means of communicating across cultures. She says that, "In most businesses people are promoted into management because they have good technical skills. The problem is they have no people skills. This problem is compounded when a manager must interact with colleagues and subordinates who are culturally different." By focusing on cultural diversity the discipline of sociology prepares people to better understand those with whom they come into contact. This is as much a skill as being able to process data statistically.

While still working on her Ph.D. Janique and a friend decided to pool their interests and resources in order to create a business. The focus of this business is to provide an array of consultative services to business organizations. Janique has primary responsibility for organizational research, which includes survey research, administering focus groups, overseeing training, and instrumentation. The objective of Janique's consultations is to help a business develop its human resource. For example, through "executive coaching" a CEO can come to better understand the problems of communication which cross over levels of work. Or, through a special training seminar personnel in constant contact with business clients can learn how to be more flexible regarding client needs. These cases focus on developing an organizational actor's perspective rather than their technical skills.

As an example consider the following summary of a sales seminar conducted for insurance sales agents. The initial question asked was, "What is your product?" In response most sales agents answered, "My insurance policies." This sounds reasonable enough on the surface. However, below the surface you find another way of looking at the "product." The sales agents were asked if the kinds of insurance policies which various companies offered was common knowledge? They replied that agents were highly familiar with competition policies because in the industry policies are very similar from company to company. The agents were then asked the following question, "Given the similarity of policies in the industry, why should a potential client buy your particular policy?" After some discussion the conclusion is that a client's choice will be influenced primarily by the relationship to the agent. This then focuses the sales question on how the agent-client relationship is conducted. One implication suggested by this is that the agent's real product -- the thing the agent actually produces -- is an effective relationship, and not the insurance policy only. Viewed in this way the critical variable is the human resource. And, proper development of that resource, including development of the sales agent's own perspective, is critical to business success.

Janique also does work enhancing social perspective and human development on a variety of other fronts. The following is a partial rundown on the issues and topics which are addressed as human resource development. It is the case that business is more global now than ever before. As a result, business people from different parts of the world must somehow find common ground on which to work. There are two ways in which this can happen. One is international business relations conducted between two separate companies. The other is inter-organizational relations conducted between international divisions of the same multinational corporation such as AT&T. One of the most problematic variables of such relations is language. In any context, and especially a business context, it is threatening to not know what is being said because you do not understand the language being spoken. It suggests the possibility of secrets, and therefore unreliable relationships. As a case in point, the United States is the fourth largest Spanish-speaking country in the world. Yet, how many businesses are prepared to incorporate Spanish-speaking employees, clients, etc.?

Other issues Janique consults on are related to gender, minorities, people with disabilities, and age discrimination. In each case Janique seeks to help the organization interpret people, defined by these categories, as assets rather than liabilities. She does this with the following model. She begins with in-depth interviews designed to frame the issues. Typically, people tend to experience problems at the interpersonal level. The result is that the organizational response is often to micro-manage the situation. Since the objective is to produce macro-leadership it is necessary to redefine the interpersonal-level problem. This is done by generating broader awareness of the issue through seminars. It is also important to involve critical organizational actors because they have influence on the definitional process. General approaches at raising awareness are followed up with training designed to change behavior. Since macro-leadership is the objective, it is important to coalesce the employees of a business into a team. If they do not see the common ground then real change is not probable. Focus groups are one mechanism for accomplishing this as employees themselves negotiate the issues and take ownership. By making resolution the responsibility of everyone, then ownership is produced. Where necessary this process is reinforced with one-on-one training, executive coaching, and even having a "hot line" for immediate private talks.

When asked, Janique says that business is good. The fact is, change must be expected in both society and its organization. The result is that there is always a need for adaptation to new circumstances. Since it is easy for a business to be focused primarily on its technical existence, it will always need help in also focusing on social and cultural adaptation processes.

Once Janique's business has successfully completed a consultation on social change with a company the ground work is thus laid for future referrals. In fact, most future consultations with other companies are the result of referrals. Taken together these referrals and contacts constitute a valuable network. Janique refers to this network as "strategic alliances." These alliances put her consultant business in position to take advantage of information flows and developing trends. For example, being a part of the American Management Association (a professional society) keeps Janique's business in touch with the issues on which she may later consult.

Janique wants undergraduate students to know that there is a bright future in the type of professional work she performs. However, it does take initiative, creativity, and a sound basis in research. But it also requires clarity in the techniques of business. Therefore, Janique suggests that students be broadly prepared, maybe earning a dual major like business and sociology, so that they can operate in both environments. For this reason internships are highly recommended.

Finally, if one's consultant business is good, as Janique's is, what does it mean for income? Janique says it all depends on how busy you are and what kinds of work you are doing. However, as an example, on-site consultations usually run $175 - $200 per day, plus expenses. This alone translates into annual salaries of $40,000 plus.

The point of Janique's experience is, it is possible with the right preparation, to work independently with degrees in sociology. Sociology provides a much needed perspective and a set of skills which can earn you a living in the world of corporations.

NOTE:
For more information important to this career see the following chapters in
Sociology: A Down to Earth Approach, by James M. Henslin:

Chapter 2 Culture
Chapter 6 Social Groups: Societies to Social Networks
Chapter 7 Bureaucracy and Formal Organizations
Chapter 11 Inequalities of Gender
Chapter 12 Inequalities of Race and Ethnicity
Chapter 14 The Economy: Money and Work

5.

SOCIOLOGY AND CAREERS
IN FEDERAL GOVERNMENT

Randy Jackson came to sociology after a long and circuitous journey. Perhaps even more interesting, Randy works for the IRS; that's the Internal Revenue Service! There is a certain atypicality in Randy's career, both its path and its destination, and that is something Randy wants others to know.

"There is not a typical career path anymore. Yes, there are people whose careers have developed predictably, but these people tend to be at the end of their work lives. And their work life is not a realistic model for people now entering the work force. " Randy says that, "Change is the watchword, and sociology is one of the few disciplines which addresses change head on."

It is not enough to simply anticipate that some kind of change will occur. According to Randy, you must be more proactive than that. Waiting on change to strike could easily leave you totally out of the picture. "One must actively participate in creating or `designing' change. In this way you can influence how change will affect you and those around you. "When reviewing Randy's "career" it is easy to see how he has come to this point of view. Randy's college and early adult life took shape during the 1960's when major social movements shook the nation. As important as the changes themselves was Randy's development of skills of questioning and applying the critical eye to any social norm or structure. Randy's undergraduate degree was in history, and one year later he earned an M.A., also in history. If it were not for the phenomenon of change, then history, as a discipline, would lose much, if not all of its value. In its place tradition would suffice. It was in history that Randy first began considering the broad scope of societal change. And, he was living it during the civil rights movement of the 1960's. It was in the living of it that Randy came to some dissatisfaction with academic history. The scope was too broad. He wanted to "take hold of the trends, the patterns, the personal styles of people. It was important to exercise some influence over them. "

After earning his master's degree Randy served in Vietnam. There he saw another example of how people can easily be caught up in patterns, and changes to those patterns, that they do not understand. His role in army administration provided opportunity to make changes, but he lacked training or understanding of the process. After his discharge Randy enrolled for a short time in seminary. Here one could begin dealing with the ultimate "whys" of social values and processes, if not with the "hows." While

23.

seminary may have been helpful in some regards, it did not deal sufficiently with the specific social processes which Randy wanted to get his hands on.

Randy quit seminary and enrolled in a special IRS administrative intern program. This move was not directly correlated to his past educational experience, but Randy did have administrative experience in the army. In this internship Randy received specialized training in labor relations, personnel relations, human resource management, and work design. Here Randy could see the real impact of work on people's lives, and that he could have a professional and fulfilling career in work design. Completion of the internship led to employment with the IRS. However, encountering the problems and issues of IRS administration led Randy back to school where he earned his Ph.D. in sociology, with a focus on organization and occupations.

As a human resource manager Randy is constantly trying to adjust the organization, the IRS, in ways that benefit both the individual and the organization. For example, Randy works at developing the idea of work as an occupation. According to Randy, "If you have 10,000 computer operators within the organization, and they have no sense of common occupation, then you simply have 10,000 individual employees. This can be a most difficult situation because the organization, and its administration, depends significantly on the self-organization that a real sense of occupation can instill in a worker." What this means is that as a member of an occupation an individual worker is always "connected" to other workers who have the same work experiences. Because of this network workers can help each other find their way around an organization, they can educate each other regarding specific work skills, or they can simply share their feelings, even their gripes, about their work. But beyond this, the idea of occupation conveys both identity and structural position. Perhaps the best way to understand these two concepts is to illustrate them in the negative.

The first piece of information we often seek about someone is their name. The next piece of information we seek is occupation. Now, assume you have no job, or you have just lost one. What happens? You feel a lack of identity. The point is, according to Randy, "Our occupation becomes part of our identity. Therefore, we must take care of how occupations are defined and managed." Perhaps even more importantly, "We must be careful when occupations are poorly managed because it is possible that a significant portion of one's identity could be lost. This is much more than organizational development, it is human development."

A second concept, structural position, refers to how the occupation fits into the broader organization. According to Randy, "Too often people see a job as a set of tasks, such as operating a computer or some other machine. An occupation gives you a role within the organization, and you begin to see just how your specific job fits in with the rest of the work being done." Such a perspective influences all kinds of work-life experiences, like interdepartmental cooperation. For example, imagine the ability of some company's administration to function without the constant contributions of physical plant staff, including janitorial and maintenance.

For that matter, how would a manager function without assistants or secretaries? The point is, each occupation has a role to play, and a clear understanding of that role is essential to fulfillment of that role.

In general it is Randy's job to see to it that all of these aspects of occupation are made functional within the IRS. He does this in a surprisingly wide variety of ways. One of the most common ways is through interorganizational requests. One kind of request is for his skill set; the other is for his perspective. According to Randy, he is "often approached by people in the organization because they have a need for some skill I have. For example, someone will want to collect data from employees on some issue and will want to conduct a survey. That's when they call me." The problem is, most people have little or no idea of what goes into survey construction and administration. "In other cases," says Randy, "someone will have data they need analyzed, but do not have the statistical background to do the analysis. Or, they may need to present some data in a report, but they have little or no idea what the data mean, let alone how to present it to others who may know even less. The point is, my methodological skills often attract others to me. I see these as opportunities to introduce my perspective, my sociological point of view on the issue at hand."

This last point, perspective or point of view, is where Randy sees his fundamental contribution. His work is usually conducted within the context of a small group of human resource managers. Others in the group are psychologists, social psychologists, and ergonomists. One thing in common about these other perspectives is the focus on the individual. To Randy this focus is much too narrow. "Often, in quick informal ways, like over lunch, I put forward my sociological perspective on whatever is up for discussion."

The critical point is that while Randy is a member of the IRS organization, an actor within it, he is also a constant observer of it. The result is a much broader perspective on behaviors within the organization and its development over time. It is in the framing of specific organizational issues that impact is achieved. Randy refers to this contribution as "situational." It is not possible to over-haul the entire organization. Randy reports that being confronted with situations in need of relatively immediate solutions, he must exercise a lot of flexibility. "There is always a lot of organizational movement swirling around you, and you are forced into making necessary decisions quickly. You do not have much time for reflection." Hence Randy's sociological perspective gives him a frame of reference for seeing and responding to the situation.

What Randy is doing in the context of the "situation" is converting the sociological perspective into a skill. The skill is in the framing of situations so that certain kinds of definitions are typically applied. This, however, requires an eclectic set of skills. When asked to advise students regarding courseware which would prepare them for his kind of work Randy's list went on and on, including, research methods, statistics,

25.

computer science, conflict resolution, change management, market research, counseling, career development, etc.! To this Randy emphasizes the need for excellent communication skills: "Without the ability to write, speak, present, or simply talk you are without the basic skills necessary to advance your point of view."

The dynamics within any organization are typical of society and its larger institutions. The result is there is always some opportunity opening up somewhere. According to Randy, this is especially true of government. If well prepared, there are plenty of employment opportunities. The B.A. level graduate in sociology definitely has a future, according to Randy, "if the emphasis is on the skills and not the title of sociologist. What people want are results, not titles." Entry level salaries range from $18,000 to $23,000 with promotions after a year advancing those salaries significantly. Graduate degrees, such as the M.A., are especially helpful and can raise salaries into the mid $40,000's. Of course, experience influences salary and Randy strongly recommends the undergraduate internship. Remember this is how Randy latched on to his job with the IRS. However, Randy's perspective on career must be understood. "The idea of a typical career path may be past." For those who are prepared and flexible the future is promising.

NOTE:

For more information important to this career see the following chapters in Sociology: A Down to Earth Approach, by James M. Henslin:

        Chapter 5 How Sociologists Do Research
        Chapter 7 Bureaucracy and Formal Organizations
        Chapter 14 The Economy: Money and Work
        Chapter 15 Politics: Power and Authority

6.

SOCIOLOGY AND CAREERS
IN URBAN SOCIAL WORK

Kent Morgan earned his degree in sociology in the mid-1980's and began pursuing his dream of Christian ministry in the inner city. This commitment was a combination of his college education and his experiences in various forms of community service. While a student Kent did social service internships and also did volunteer work within the community. For example, one of Kent's internships focused on the development of positive peer leadership among youth. Skills for developing such leadership were taught during a weekend camp. Kent began as a student observer/participant and in subsequent camps became a group leader, implementing the leadership program. At the same time Kent volunteered within the community as a soccer coach. "I didn't really know anything about soccer. I played basketball. But the kids needed a soccer coach. Besides, I checked a book out on the game and asked some of my college friends who played to help me out. We didn't win a lot of games, but we had fun. What I got out of it was a clearer sense of how I could have an impact on the lives of others."

One of the organizations with which Kent came into contact while in college was the Salvation Army. The summer after graduation Kent pursued his interest in kids by working as a unit director at a Salvation Army camp. The camp was designed for older, inner city boys, and gave them a chance to escape their environment for a while. At this camp, according to Kent, "I began to see more clearly how sociological concepts like environment and social structure could help me better understand these kids. I also saw how I could use these concepts to influence young lives. So I began to dig into the backgrounds of my kids, and I even visited some of them in their homes some months later. I was really interested in these boys, and they needed hope for the future. The camp experience was great, but it was only short term. I knew I wanted to do something for them in their home environment."

Kent decided to follow his developing interest in inner city youth by seeking permanent employment with the Salvation Army. He applied and was offered a job as a community center social worker with a case load of 150 families. In this job Kent was responsible for a wide range of family services, with a special focus on children and youth. The array of services included, but was not limited to individual counseling, crisis intervention, energy service to homes, finding shelter, serving as a liaison with police, etc. According to Kent, "You get to be quite close to these people. You can see the product of your efforts. There was much that was frustrating, but also much more that was rewarding."

As Kent's work at the community center progressed he took on the position of community services director. This position broadened Kent's perspective. In his four years at the center Kent was responsible for proposing, developing, and implementing 18 new programs. These programs, according to Kent, were "based on a holistic approach to problem solving. My background in sociology really provided a valuable framework for approaching my job. Specifically, this framework forced me to look into the larger community for patterns which were contributing to the problems we saw arising in individual cases. We had hunches, but we also needed data so we could reasonably respond. Therefore, any program development had to include research."

One example of how Kent applied his perspective was development of the Young Conquerors program. A significant and obvious problem in his part of the city was gang activity and delinquency. What was not so obvious was how people perceived the problem and what should be done about it. Through extensive interviews with people from the local community, including gang members and potential gang members, Kent determined that gang members were the primary role models for children. There were no real alternatives. Further, and interestingly, role models from the gangs were not necessarily preferred by current or potential members. The task was to create a class of new, alternative role models/leaders among the youth. This was done by involving youth and community leaders alike in structures which promoted and rewarded appropriate behavior. Activities like organized sports and volunteer services were actively promoted. When certain young people were successful in these endeavors then it became their responsibility to reproduce their success through the lives of others. According to Kent, "Being a role model/leader is more than simply being someone others admire. It carries with it the responsibility for advancing the lives of others."

After four years Kent decided to go into full time Salvation Army ministry and therefore went back to school, this time seminary. His desire was to be of more help to people spiritually. Yet, as Kent notes, "I recognized that in order to help people spiritually I needed to better my understanding of people socially." So, in addition to his master's level seminary degree in theology Kent also pursued a Ph.D. in counseling and became licensed as a social worker in two states. According to Kent, "My life is dedicated to helping people help themselves, so my commitment must be to understanding people as thoroughly as possible."

After His seminary studies were completed Kent was commissioned as a Salvation Army Officer and took on the dual position of chief administrator and head pastor in, what has turned out to be, a most challenging community. "This is an intimidating place," says Kent. "There are high rates of drug abuse, gang activity, teenage pregnancy, child and elder abuse, etc. What's worse, people don't seem to have any idea what to do about it. It's a big part of my job to give definition to those problems, seek and develop solutions, and engage the community in implementation." To this end Kent has relied heavily upon his research skills. He has conducted at least three demographic studies to get a clear picture of the community he is serving. He has also conducted needs assessments, to determine where to act and in what priority. He is engaged in strategic planning so that both his organization and the community know and understand the future towards which they are heading. And, he had begun to use all this research to access outside resources. On two occasions he has successfully applied for grants which have established needed programs.

For example, within the last year he was awarded $56,000 for a growth enrichment initiative. For young people ages 14-18, this program provides valuable learning experiences in three areas; academic, life-skills/employment, and recreation/leisure. For two years these young people are actually students in courses designed to help them better organize and advance their lives. Successful completion of the curriculum also results in college credit through the local community college district. "We are just getting ready to graduate our first class!" says a rightfully proud Kent. "Had I not been able to organize the data and write coherently then this program would not be here, and we would have no graduates today."

Understanding his community sociologically is an asset Kent wonders how people in his position can do without. But his skills are also directed organizationally. He oversees a staff of ten which he motivates to work aggressively. He must also continually network with the rest of the community. He must build relational bridges, so his management and communication skills are always being tested. According to Kent, "You can't rest in this job for two reasons. One, as a representative of the Salvation Army I am always 'on stage'. People have certain expectations of me and I must live up to them, or change them, if I am to have any legitimacy. Two, the environment is always in flux. Change is always a part of what we must address. As soon as you deal with one problem another emerges. But, my holistic point of view helps me to anticipate change."

Financially, Kent wants it known that he is "comfortable." He is not in the ministry to make money, but to serve others. As an entry level social worker he made $17,000+ ten years ago. Now, with a package that includes a home and a car, Kent earns $55,000 - $60,000 annually. "I'm able to do the work I feel called to do, and provide for my family as well. I am blessed."

NOTE
For more information important to this career see the following chapters in
Sociology: A Down to Earth Approach, by James M. Henslin:
>Chapter 5 How Sociologists Do Research
>Chapter 8 Deviance and Social Control
>Chapter 10 Social Class in American Society
>Chapter 18 Religion: Establishing Meaning
>Chapter 20 Population and Urbanization

7.

SOCIOLOGY AND CAREERS
IN THE MILITARY

During college Karen Jensen took only one undergraduate course in sociology. Her major was biology and she took the sociology course because, "I needed an 'A'! I wasn't much interested in the social sciences. I saw my future in medicine, as a nurse." After graduation Karen took a job as a nurse in a hospital and worked there for the next six to seven years. Within the structures of the hospital she reached the level of Unit Manager on the EMT floor. Her work was primarily administration, with responsibility for primary care nurses, supplies, equipment, etc. "In this position I became very much aware of the importance of organizational issues as they impacted our efforts to deliver health care. You see, a hospital can be its own society. It is very hierarchical with doctors and nurses occupying well defined roles. There is also a lot of cross-disciplinary interaction. Because of this people in hospitals sometimes have difficulty relating. This creates very interesting organizational dynamics."

It is clear that Karen was no longer working strictly within the confines of her nursing degree. As with so many of today's careers, Karen's on-the-job experiences had given her responsibilities which she had not anticipated. The lesson here is that one should anticipate, and not be surprised by such developments.

As Karen's career developed her administrative responsibilities increased. If she was to continue in this direction she felt the need for additional education.   Her first choice was industrial/organizational psychology. However, as she explored other possibilities she found in organizational sociology a "helpful understanding, or framing, of the issues at work." She also found a discipline which was highly flexible. She noted that, "There are so many directions you can go and subspecialities which you can study." Within sociology Karen found opportunities to study research methods, statistics and computer applications. Topically, Karen studied formal organizational theory, management, organization and power, and medical sociology. She was also introduced to a variety of social issues, such as cultural diversity.

The flexibility and variety within sociology meant that Karen could follow her interests and design her own degree path. She reported that, "At times this freedom could be a bit overwhelming. You have to take hold of the discipline, and of yourself, in order to bring closure to open-ended programs. But the multiple advantages outweigh this disadvantage." One specific advantage was the opportunity to apply the discipline to her work in the hospital which she stayed involved with for the first part of her M.A. studies. Karen culminated her M.A. with a thesis on the changing role of nurses. As a nurse and sociologist Karen was in a unique position to study this topic. Obviously this is a topic of some significance given that we all encounter health care through a nurse. Their role is critical, and it is to our advantage to better understand how the work of the nurse is constructed. The result of this was an M.A. in the sociology of organization, work, and occupation, with a subspecialty in medical sociology.

For Karen the graduate school experience was sometimes awkward. She had been employed full-time for a number of years before returning to school, and the transition produced some role confusion. "At work," she said, "I was a unit manager. In school I was somewhat of an adolescent. I wanted to continue on for the Ph.D., but I was also ready to go back to work. So, I began looking for research positions in the paper and tech journals, and I put the word out to my friends that I was looking. Over the years I had developed an extensive network of contacts, and I hoped that this might turn something up." The network did turn something up, but it was an opportunity wholly unanticipated. "A friend of mine used to work for the Military Department of Research (MDR), and she helped arrange an interview. Now you must understand that working for the military would have been the last choice on my list. I knew nothing about the military, and my impressions were not all that favorable."

There was a job at MDR, originally written as a research psychologist, but re-written for a research sociologist. The emphasis within the job description was on the skills of the discipline of sociology--the methods, the processing of data, the manipulation of statistics. Little or no emphasis was given to the perspectives sociology offers. What Karen brought with her was a high degree of skill in producing and managing data, programming experience in SPSS (Statistical Package for the Social Sciences), a facility in writing, and a demonstrated ability to learn. She noted that, "The ability to learn is perhaps the most important variable in this job. Once on the job the necessary learning curve is very steep. You have to be able to pick up on what is happening. You have to be able to adjust."

What is especially interesting is that Karen did not have to demonstrate a foreknowledge of military matters to be of service and to contribute effectively. The discipline of sociology supported her in two ways: in the technical skills, which are universally applicable, and her sociological perspective which helps her to adapt. "I use my sociology both on projects to which I am assigned and as a way of conducting myself within the organization. While I am still a bit uncomfortable with military culture--for example, all the acronym talk--I am nonetheless always observing it and adapting to it. I am also contributing to it within my own sphere of influence."

A major project in which Karen has been involved has focused on the military family. In what ways do military families influence the functioning of military personnel? In what ways does the military affect the families of military personnel? How does the family respond to critical events, like Desert Storm? In pursuit of answers to these and related questions, Karen has spent a lot of time constructing and administering surveys, conducting interviews, processing the data produced, and writing up findings. Ultimately this research produces recommendations, and it is here that Karen sees real contributions in her work.

Karen wants undergraduates studying sociology to know that in applied work, like her's, "There is always an agenda with which you are working. There is no academic vacuum for research. We are constantly being asked to find the answers to some questions." This is her job. But she says, "We also have to find out what the real question behind the initial question is." For example, "Our agenda item in the military research into family is the `prospect to re-enlist' of military personnel. Taking better care of military families may produce a more durable and consistent military force."

After working for a year or so at MDR Karen was able to complete her Ph.D. in sociology. She is pleased with the way things have turned out. "There are a lot of opportunities and I believe that what I do really makes a difference." Karen has also answered the concerns of her mother who said she "did not see a future in sociology," and often confused it with social work. Karen now earns an annual income of $40,000 - $50,000. Entry level positions, with advanced degrees pay at $30,000 - $40,000. According to Karen, "I make a comfortable living, and I have a lot of work freedom. More importantly, I enjoy what I am doing."

NOTE:

For more information important to this career see the following chapters in Sociology: A Down to Earth Approach, by James M. Henslin:

Chapter 5 How Sociologists Do Research
Chapter 7 Bureaucracy and Formal Organizations
Chapter 15 Politics: Power and Authority
Chapter 16 The Family: Our Introduction to Society

8.

SOCIOLOGY AND CAREERS
IN STATE GOVERNMENT

Hal Jackson had an interest in teaching and pursued a rather straightforward academic path, earning B.A., M.A., and Ph.D. degrees, all in sociology. His initial intent had been to teach, but his "love of the mountains" took him to a location where teaching jobs were scarce. However, during his studies Hal had emphasized and developed his research methods and quantitative skills, which he used in order to pursue employment in non-academic sociology.

Since teaching was not an immediate option, his first step was to look for "research" positions with governmental and quasi-governmental agencies. While in his Ph.D. program Hal had became familiar with a number of such agencies. "It is the case," according to Hal, "that agencies within government are always working on projects which require data gathering, analysis, and/or interpretation. If you are well-trained then you can stay quite busy."

The second step Hal took was to take a state test to qualify him as a "researcher." Together these two steps opened several doors. Hal reported that, "The degree in sociology was especially important in getting the attention of people who were hiring researchers. It opened numerous doors." However, having a degree was not enough. According to Hal, "you have to be able to produce. Ultimately, people are less interested in your degree than if you can do the job."

These job search efforts led Hal on a career "path" that would have been difficult to anticipate in its full detail. He was offered a job in criminology where he did monitoring and evaluation research on federally funded programs. Hal says that, "Nearly all federal programs have an evaluation mechanism built into them. The question is whether the program is really accomplishing its objectives. My state, and the governor in particular, were interested in violent offenders and appropriate state responses." For example, community corrections was developing at this time as an alternative to imprisonment. While good in theory, citizens and politicians wanted to know how effective community-based correction programs were. Hal became involved in all aspects of research on this problem, from the development of program measures (how to quantify the issues and define the problems), to data collection (interviews, survey construction and administration), data processing (interpretation of results), and the preparation of reports.

Hal's effective work on this crime treatment project led to a second project within the area of criminal justice. Due to rising prices the energy industry was beginning to exploit and develop western oil reserves, particularly shale oil One result of this was the growth of "boom towns." The idea of a boom town is that its development is sudden, and often without careful anticipation or study of its effects. One critical problem in boom towns is crime. Since people are rapidly moving into a boom town the social structure usually cannot develop fast enough to handle all issues and/or problems. City government, for example, may not be able to keep up with the need or demand for police protection.

Hal's second project was to collect data and publish ethnographic reports on the nature of boom towns and crime within them. This included not only descriptions of criminals and victims, but also the local community's reaction to crime. Such research has far-reaching effects. If widespread economic development is defined as "good" for the state then protection of that good would be essential. If boom town crime were not adequately addressed then the economic development represented by the boom towns themselves might be curtailed or even reversed. How could you get skilled people to move to a location where crime was known to be a problem? Hal's research problem was thus defined.

Eventually, funding for the criminal justice projects began to run out and Hal moved into another sector of state government. This time he was working for the state auditor's office doing performance auditing. Networking was a key to getting this job, but networking was also a significant benefit of it. As a performance auditor Hal found himself meeting personally with most of the rest of the departments in state government. In state government agencies there are often multiple agendas and many competing, interests. There are the interests of those who seek some service, the interests of those who have lobbied effectively for providing that service, the interests of those who work within the agency, the interests of those who directly provide the service, and the interests of all those who would like to see the agency or service cut or curtailed because of tight money. What is important here, according to Hal, is that good data are produced so that sound judgments can be made. "Unfortunately," according to Hal, "there is simply a lot of poor research and bad data floating around." Poor research can lead to the funding of ineffective programs or perhaps, more critically, the termination of effective programs. Concludes Hal, "Methodological clarity is absolutely essential, and sociology is one discipline which can provide this."

One of the current trends in government is "restructuring." "Because Hal had worked in several state agencies, and because his work, particularly as a performance auditor, had exposed him to many departments of state government and to many leaders in the state, he had become deeply informed on the workings of state agencies. He also had front-line evaluation experience, so he knew the critical questions to ask. His networking meant that he had formal and informal contacts throughout government. And finally, he knew how to do good research. Hal noted that, "Change is the watchword in restructing, and my background in sociology is perfect for understanding change. There are so many variables, and so many people with interests in what you do that you must be able to see the big picture. Restructing is impossible with a narrowly focused point of view. Our objective," said Hal, "is to provide more and better services to our clients--citizens of this state--with less money. Good information is absolutely essential if good decisions are to be made."

Hal's perspective on the value of sociology does not end with evaluation. He reported that, "Somehow we must be able to present to the public what we are trying to do. That takes excellent communication skills, both written and oral. Further, we must be able to work together. Only as teams can we accomplish our objectives." In other words, Hal must be versed in a variety of skills, all of which are fundamentally sociological. When asked to describe what he actually does in his work, Hal gave the following list: he plans, collects information, communicates, leads teams, helps manage through the decision process, acts as a catalyst, translates "bureaucratese" into words for the average citizen, lobbies, etc., etc. And, all this must be done in real time with real and immediate deadlines. Hal also noted that, "You have to be able to compose on the computer or you'll simply not get the work done." In all of these pursuits according the Hal, "The importance of one's network keeps surfacing as being paramount. The kinds of judgments people make about you when you are not around is essential to the success of your work."

Taken together it can be said that Hal has had a career. In fact Hal has, but not in a traditional sense of holding a job for twenty years. He has moved from a $25,000 per year agency researcher to a $65,000 per year state government manager with wide-ranging responsibilities. He also teaches part-time (his original goal) and earns an additional $9,000-$10,000 per year. So far Hal says he has "no regrets," and looks forward to the new challenges which will most certainly come his way. His choice to follow nonacademic pursuits has "opened up a whole new world" to him. For students following Hal's path, his career is quite encouraging. However, students must be proactive in their pursuit. They must be flexible and seek a variety of hands-on experiences. Hal's advice is for undergraduate students to, "take temporary jobs, do practicums and internships, and volunteer. See for yourself how your discipline applies."

NOTE:

For more information important to this career see the following chapters in Sociology: A Down to Earth Approach, by James M. Henslin:

> Chapter 5 How Sociologists Do Research
> Chapter 7 Bureaucracy and Formal Organizations
> Chapter 15 Politics: Power and Authority
> Chapter 21 Collective Behavior and Social Movements

9.

SOCIOLOGY AND CAREERS
IN CRIMINAL JUSTICE

Pat Eklund graduated with an undergraduate degree in sociology and several hundred hours of "time" spent as an intern in a local state correctional facility. According to Pat, "That time and those experiences in prison have been the springboard for my career in criminal justice. I was being prepared in ways that I did not know or understand at the time; and I am even now still discovering the lessons I learned then." Underlying these experiences was his sociological perspective. Many people can occupy the same context and experience the same situation, but what they "see" in that situation is dependent upon what they are prepared to see. "I am always looking for why things happen, what's underneath someone's behavior. This is where my degree in sociology has proved invaluable," concluded Pat.

Since graduation five years ago Pat has made steady progress within the broad field of criminal justice. Pat began his career by working with children who were wards of the state for various reasons. For this residential program Pat had been prepared by research he had conducted while a correctional intern. As an intern Pat had an opportunity to focus on the prison intake process, including opportunities to examine background files. Pat reported that, "In these files I discovered common juvenile histories, most of which evidenced significant family problems. This led to my first job with children where I hoped to have some influence during this critical stage of development."

After about a year Pat moved more directly into criminal justice when he took a job with a county juvenile home. Here Pat worked with juveniles referred or sentenced by a juvenile court. "These were kids whose next stop would very likely be an adult correctional facility. Just like many of the young guys I processed while an intern." In this position Pat began to realize how much social contextual variables influenced the life opportunities of the young people with whom he was working. "I came to the conclusion that these kids and their families needed to be reached before the kids were sent to a juvenile facility." For Pat this meant getting closer to the community and for him to work in law enforcement as a police officer.

In the last three years Pat has worked as a county sheriff's deputy; and presently he is a city police officer. "My objective," said Pat, "was to be a police officer in a town or city. This way I could begin to apply my academic preparation in sociology to the larger problems of community life." As a county officer Pat was not able to focus his work on any one locale, and therefore was always encountering new situations. But, as Pat noted, "As a community police officer I am in a position to study the smaller patterns as well as the larger structures which influence lives. In one sense I feel like a participant-observer. I am a police officer, but I'm constantly observing like a sociologist. In fact, there is very little about being a police officer that is not enhanced by seeing things as a sociologist."

For example, Pat describes the domestic disturbance as one of the most frequent and, potentially, one of the most dangerous calls to which police respond. "Unfortunately too many officers make a bad situation worse by the way they have already defined domestic disturbances. If you assume ahead of time that these problems are always the fault of the husband, father, or boyfriend, then everything you will do as an officer will target that person. What happens is that the person targeted (the husband, for example) senses this right away and can become afraid or defensive. This is when a bad situation can become worse, which might even mean dangerous." Body language is one variable which Pat now emphasizes. This would include keeping an open body posture with arms at the side instead of folded. The point, according to Pat, "is that when there is a family problem there is always more than one point of view, and there is usually legitimacy in each person's definition. You have to communicate that you are willing to listen to all sides of the issue."

One of the larger structural issues a criminal justice professional should know is how the community is arranged according to socioeconomic status, ethnic identity, and age. Each of these variables is especially important for understanding specific conflict situations. Pat notes, "It is always important to understand the effects of stereotypes on how people perceive a community problem. And it's important to know when you are simply confronting a stereotype in the line of your work. For example, witnesses to a crime will overwhelmingly describe the criminal as male or minority. But by asking questions carefully you are able to get a more meaningful description, often one at odds with the minority variable."

It is also important to understand that a community is composed of relational networks. According to Pat, "I actually seek out the networks because it is through them that I can stay in touch with what is happening. Knowing these networks is like understanding the family. Each has its own pattern and priorities. And it is here that the lives of young people can really be influenced. Hopefully, they can be influenced before they end up being institutionalized."

So far we have seen how Pat has applied his studies in sociology to his work in criminal justice. And, we have seen that Pat has launched a reasonable career path. Three general questions remain. What kind of income can one expect with this career path? Is the undergraduate degree in sociology sufficient education? What recommendations does Pat offer to those who might be inclined to follow in his footsteps?

38.

Pat's income has been steady over the five years since his graduation. His children's home job paid approximately $17,000 per year, while the county juvenile home paid approximately $22,000 per year. His first job in law enforcement as a county sheriff's deputy paid about $20,000. In his first year as a city police officer his base salary was approximately $33,000, with overtime and extra duties adding up to $5,000 more. Pat is quick to note that police salaries do vary according to community size and region. In his case, Pat sees his income as "quite livable."

The undergraduate degree in sociology was "absolutely right" for the career he has had, and anticipates having, according to Pat. The internships proved especially valuable in securing the first jobs. While no longer at the youth homes these jobs provided Pat with an opportunity "to test my ideas." Pat was able both to learn from these positions, and to set his future course from what he had learned. Had he gone directly into law enforcement Pat suggests he might not have been as well prepared as he is now. Yet, all aspects of his career are tied to his undergraduate preparations in sociology. Pat notes that, "While I have had several different job titles, applied sociology is what I do." Among other things Pat now sees himself as especially adaptable. "I was prepared by my degree for the necessity of continued learning and adaptation to change."

For those considering a career in the broad field of criminal justice Pat has some advice. He says that the idea of continuous learning and adaptability suggests that persons entering the field of criminal justice should be prepared to complete additional formal learning. In each job Pat has either been required to take additional training or has chosen to do so. For example, prior to assuming his sheriff's deputy duties Pat was enrolled in a twelve-week academy. Interestingly, Pat suggests that only about 25% of the academy focused on specifically legal issues or practices such as knowing legal codes, weapons, etc. The most significant work of the academy was preparing future officers for dealing with people. He observed that, "We spent a lot of time role-playing and modeling people's behavior. Group dynamics were continuously stressed." In addition, emphasis was given to emerging issues of cultural diversity. According to Pat, "If you want to go into law enforcement you need to learn that there are other patterns of living, and it is up to the officer to adapt."

Aside from the academy there are many types of continuing - education opportunities and/or requirements. Recently Pat attended a seminar on interviewing and interrogation. The distinctions are important and require different kinds of officer-subject relations. When questioned about promotion Pat reported that additional formal education would be required. For example, a Master's of Criminal Justice degree would qualify one for a chief or department chief position. Interestingly, many current criminal justice programs have had their origins in sociology departments!

For those considering a career in the broad field of criminal justice Pat offers the following recommendations. Focus on degree programs which emphasize human relations. For this he said, sociology is a natural.

39.

You must understand cultural diversity and be adaptable to different cultural contexts. Foreign language capability, especially Spanish, is nearly essential. Other languages are emphasized according to local needs. For example, southeast Asian languages (Vietnamese, Laotian, Cambodian, Chinese, etc.) are needed in areas like California. In Los Angeles alone 186 different languages and dialects are spoken! Computer literacy is a must. Pat now has a lap-top computer in his squad car. He composes his written reports quickly and these are transmitted directly and immediately to the department for analysis. This way there is no lag-time between an event and the recording of that event. Obviously, assumed by this development is the need for good writing-skills. Oral communication is also essential if one is to conduct good community relations. In other words, all the skills developed within a degree in sociology are skills essential to a career in criminal justice. Finally, Pat strongly recommends internships. "It is in the internship that you begin to make the connections between your courseware and your career."

NOTE:
For more information important to this career see the following chapters in
Sociology: A Down to Earth Approach, by James M. Henslin:

Chapter 4	Social Structure and Social Interaction:
	Macrosociology and Microsociology
Chapter 6	Social Groups: Societies to Social Networks
Chapter 8	Deviance and Social Control
Chapter 10	Social Class in American Society
Chapter 16	The Family: Our Introduction to Society

10.

SOCIOLOGY AND CAREERS
IN SEMINARAND WORKSHOP CONSULTATIONS

Donna Holling's life and her career are a testament to perseverance, determination, and a love of learning. Now retired after 25 years of government service, Donna has developed a second career as an independent consultant - trainer. In her work for the federal government, through involvement in her church, and through her children Donna has been a real pioneer in the Black and Women's movements. Because of this she is highly networked, with a positive reputation which often precedes her. The result is that work comes looking for her.

In Donna's case, the relationship of career and sociology is less a matter of academic degree than it is a combination of significant life experiences and pursuit of education. The discipline is important in that it is compatible with her experiences. Sociology has provided skills, both hard and soft, which help Donna better understand her experiences. Thus while Donna's degree is a B.A. in sociology, it has had the impact of more advanced degrees.

After completing high school Donna's dream was to attend college. Finances prevented this and she had to go to work. Nonetheless she persisted and enrolled in a local college's night school program, part-time, and began taking courses towards a degree in criminology. In this area of study Donna encountered two "excellent" professors in sociology who helped shape her long-term academic interests. To pay the bills Donna took a day job at the college which she held for four years. However, the college did not offer a complete degree program through its night school, so her education could not be finished. Donna then took a clerical job with the IRS (Internal Revenue Services). Unfortunately, reorganization within the IRS soon cost Donna her job. But this was the early days of the civil rights movement and Donna saw that opportunities were there for those, as she said, who were "aggressive enough to go after them." Her aggressive action was to "take my case to Washington D.C. and see if those in government really meant what they said about civil rights." There the IRS rehired her at "the lowest grade level." Twenty-five years later Donna retired from government service at the highest senior executive level.

Donna's career is a classic "feel good" success story. Yet she still clung to her dream of earning a degree. She had taken some occasional courseware, but nothing in a degree track. According to Donna, "I always wanted to pursue the degree. I wanted to feel good about myself, and be able to do good for others." At this time a university in the Washington,

D.C. area was offering a unique program called University Without Walls. The idea was to award credit based on life experiences and then complete a degree with formal courseware. To determine how her life experiences would translate into college credit Donna wrote a thesis on herself, her work, and observations about the world. In addition to credit the thesis served to direct her studies into the field of sociology. But why sociology?

According to Donna the choice was sociology because in many ways it defined her own life. "It seemed that my whole life has been spent working with people in groups--my work, my children and their groups like girl scouts, my church, and other organizations. And, I have often been involved with people of various cultures and backgrounds. I have had to learn how to get along with many different people in many different settings. Sociology just seemed to fit those experiences so well. Further, sociology helped me gain a better understanding, a better feel for what was happening."

One obvious characteristic of sociology as a discipline is its wide applicability. There are also many subspecialities in sociology. Working in government for 25 years gave Donna special insight into the realities of power, and the structures in which power is exercised. Because of this Donna focused her courseware on the sociology of politics and power. On this basis, according to Donna, she would be able to "stand back from my experiences in order to see how things work from a different perspective. Sometimes when you are in the middle of a situation it is difficult to see clearly how things are really happening." This capacity of sociology to help one gain perspective provided the foundation for Donna's second career.

Donna's second career is that of independent consultant and trainer. In 25 years of government service Donna said that she became "quite well networked. Beyond people I know there are people I have heard about, and there are people who have heard about me. This is absolutely necessary for the kind of work I do." And that work is to help people in work settings begin to see their work, and the other relationships which swirl around work, from a sociological point of view. Donna says that, "If I can do this, then these people can apply the discipline for themselves, and in ways that are most important to them."

Donna's consultations and training sessions often take the form of workshops. These workshops cover a wide range of topics, including cultural diversity, women and organizational creativity, and power and organization. According to Donna, "My sociology comes into play in two ways. First, the discipline helps me see and understand the issue, such as cultural diversity in the workplace. Secondly, the discipline also helps me to administer the seminars themselves. You have to carefully manage them or you'll lose the participants." One way to run such seminars is to involve the participants in the phenomenon being examined. For example, Donna often does executive training for new CEO's or upper-level managers. The objective is to demonstrate to them that their real task is to effectively communicate what they want others to do. "So, I give them some very

42.

basic assignments. One might be to amuse a child with simple things. What they learn right away is that they have to see things from the child's point of view, not their own. Another might be to write the directions for making a peanut butter sandwich. You would be surprised at how many people forget to collect the ingredients in their instructions. The point is, they don't have a useful perspective. It's my job to help them develop one."

Donna understands that workshop participants will have some kind of perspective on whatever the issue for the workshop is. Further, Donna understands that these perspectives "have been produced over a long period of time. People aren't born with these ideas, they are put together over time. This means that they will not change quickly, but it does mean that they do and can change." For example, if women or minorities are being subjected to various kinds of discrimination or harassment, then their productivity, as employees, will certainly be affected. Donna asks, "Are we just going to dismiss all unproductive employees?" She answers, "That's not possible. Instead we must change the conditions of work, including the perceptions people have about female and/or minority co-workers. If the workshop is well done then the process of reconstructing damaging perceptions has begun."

For some this kind of work seems a bit difficult to grasp. To help you understand, Donna suggests an aggressive career development approach. She observes that, "Workshops like I do are an ongoing part of the business and government worlds. Simply because you haven't heard about them doesn't meant that they do not exist. Therefore, I suggest that researching the business of workshops and seminars be part of what you do as a student. You could begin by contacting convention bureaus and getting a list of industry conventions or annual meetings which have come to some cities. Then ask for convention schedules. You will see for yourself the array of workshops offered. But this is only the start. You need to pursue this in order to learn as much as you can."

Donna also has advice on skills to develop. She concludes, "Writing is absolutely important, as are speaking skills. You need to be able to present yourself, and what you have to say, so that others not only hear you, but will adopt the point of view you are offering." Donna also wants students to know that "you can make a living." Of course income will depend on the kinds of consultations you do, but Donna currently earns in the $60,000-$65,000 range annually.

Most important, Donna advises to "not give up on your dreams. I enjoy what I do. But I'm sure that 25 years ago I could not have seen myself where I am today. The fact is, your life will be full of many twists and turns, and you must be prepared to learn from them all."

NOTE:

For more information important to this career see the following chapters in
<u>Sociology: A Down to Earth Approach</u>, by James M. Henslin:

11.

SOCIOLOGY AND CAREERS
IN EDUCATION-ADMINISTRATION

Mary Whited and Matt Jackson were college classmates with similar interests, but widely varying twists in their academic and career paths. Matt was almost immediately "turned on" to sociology. His professors were good and the material interesting and challenging. He decided he wanted to major in sociology and perhaps teach in high school. With advanced degrees Matt thought he might even teach in college. Matt observed that, "Teaching sociology is not like other disciplines. The specific topics and cases are always changing. You could teach a class for twenty years and have new material each time. From a teacher's point of view this keeps the courses always fresh and interesting." But his dreams of teaching were cut short. Upon hearing of his decision to pursue sociology Matt's parents "raised some red flags." According to Matt, "My parents just saw no future with a sociology degree. They wanted me to get a safer degree. So, I ended up majoring in biology education. I was preparing to teach high school biology. However, there was a problem with this plan. After doing my student teaching I discovered I didn't really like it. At least not high school biology."

Because of this experience Matt decided he had no interest in pursuing a job teaching high school biology. While trying to figure out just what to do, Matt received a call from his college's department of admissions. He was offered a job as an admissions representative. His primary responsibility was to recruit students to the college. It was during this time that Matt decided to return to his first academic choice, sociology. According to Matt, "By this time my interest in sociology had grown and I'm sure that I had a greater appreciation of the discipline's power to interpret situations. I was in a practical setting where the product, a college recruit, was produced through the proper management of human relations. I could begin to see how the theories of the discipline actually played out in people's lives."

Matt began his return to sociology at the undergraduate level by earning a second major. He then moved on to the master's level where he earned his M.A. with research into to the experiences of minority students at small religiously affiliated colleges. In his job Matt soon found himself involved in multiple aspects of student life, from recruitment and admission to retention and graduation. "My education in sociology provided me with invaluable conceptual structures such as formal and informal networks, ingroup/outgroup, and minority/majority relations. I could see how these structures impacted the experiences students have in college. These ideas about structures were more than just abstract theories." Perhaps even more importantly, once these structures were understood and "seen" they could be intentionally adjusted or modified. A student's experience in college could be influenced by changing structures.

After several years Matt was "ready for some personal career advancement." He was heavily recruited by another college and took on the job of Director of Enrollment Services. Now, soon to become a Vice President, Matt has responsibility for nine professional and three support staff. Altogether this organization coordinates the work of admission representatives, admission of students to the college, financial aid distribution, and student retention.

Mary's interest in sociology was equal to Matt's, but she managed to pursue her degree to completion, including writing a departmental honors thesis. Her real interest was theory. While practical applications were interesting, abstract modeling was her passion. Because of circumstances Mary was unable to pursue her studies in graduate school. Instead, Mary worked at a variety of jobs including being an investigator for the adult protective service division of a county prosecutor's office and working as a computer consultant for businesses implementing new hardware and software. According to Mary, "What was interesting about each of these jobs was that while I had not been specifically prepared for them in a technical sense, I found that my background in sociology had prepared me to adapt to almost any situation. I had learned how to learn."

Specifically, Mary had learned how to translate her love of theory into practical applications. As a student Mary had often worked with theoretic models. The models represented clusters of sociological assumptions about why people behaved the way they do. "What I did was transfer the idea of modeling to my work. I would convert what I was experiencing to a model. Then I could examine the structure and see how best to approach some problem."

For example, in working for Adult Protective Services (APS) Mary often conducted training seminars for related agency personnel, such as the police. A seminar topic might be intergenerational abuse. As part of her ongoing work at APS Mary had collected data on cases of intergenerational abuse processed by her office. She then began to identify patterns and variables, such as social class and age. These patterns and variables would then be combined into an array of models which, when presented in seminars, would sensitize investigators, like the police, to signals of actual abuse. Without the models the police officer may not recognize the potential for abuse in some situation. According the Mary, "The problem is that people experience so much of their lives as a kind of chaos. They don't really see how the things that happen are interconnected. But if you have a correct picture of these interconnections you can begin uncovering the underlying reasons for what you experience. If you are going to have a real effect on people's lives, then making them aware of the larger picture--the model--is a real gift."

The same process was in evidence when Mary worked as a computer consultant. Mary noted that, "I was always working in new settings and it was necessary to be a quick learner. I had to quickly and accurately assess the organizational situation if I was to be successful. This often meant paying much more attention to the informal rather than the formal structure of the business. Once done I could then begin introducing my ideas regarding computer hardware and/or software." Mary did this kind of work in businesses as diverse as banks and manufacturing plants.

Through her consulting Mary eventually came into contact with a local four-year college. Her skills and capabilities were recognized and Mary was offered a position in the college's admissions department. Specifically she is the Associate Director of the Women's External Degree (WED) program. This is a program for women whereby they can earn college credit, outside the normal classroom, and eventually earn a bachelor's level degree. The women who enroll are non-traditional students. They are often older, have families, and are contending with more complex lives than 18-22 year olds. According to Mary, "The real task here is helping these women see the opportunity in WED. Although I must be careful to tell people when I don't think the program is right for them. Essentially, I help people reconstruct the realities they are presently living in. Most importantly I help them reconstruct how they perceive themselves."

After different academic and career paths Matt and Mary are now involved in the same type of work. Both see their studies in sociology as integral to success in that work. Research is a constant part of what they do. "If you can't process data then you simply can't make sense out of the important trends," according to Matt. If the school is not continuously sensitive to its environment then its recruitment efforts would easily be misdirected. Original research is a must for this kind of work. For example, Mary developed a survey to be completed by all prospective students. This data provided clear direction for future marketing efforts.

While Matt and Mary are at different stages in their careers, Matt as a new Vice President and Mary as a first year Associate Director, both see exciting futures. They are both constantly observant of their work, themselves, and their environment. As a result they are in a position to dictate opportunity, to some degree. They are on top of what is happening. According to Mary, "My sociological perspective is now second nature to me. With this I feel as if I can always find a way to exert influence over the situation. I am not simply waiting for something to happen to me." According to Matt, "I'm in the position I'm in because of my ability to organize and be proactive in my environment. My discipline provides me with the frameworks and skills necessary to do this."

Matt's and Mary's careers must be seen as constantly developing. Neither expected at the outset to be where they are now. Yet here they are.

And they are comfortable with both the quality of work life and financial rewards. Mary is in her first year and earns approximately $20,000. While not a lot, Mary is quick to point out, "there are many fringe benefits, especially for those who enjoy the collegiate atmosphere." Matt, with five to ten years of experience now earns $40,000 - $45,000. But more than money, they are in work which is intrinsically satisfying and for which the future is wide open.

NOTE:

For more information important to this career see the following chapters in
Sociology: A Down to Earth Approach, by James M. Henslin:
        Chapter 5 How Sociologists Do Research
        Chapter 17 Education: Transferring Knowledge and Skills
        Chapter 20 Population and Urbanization
        Chapter 22 Social Change, Technology, and the Environment

12.

SOCIOLOGY AND CAREERS
IN STATE AGENCIES

Deb Greer is a management analyst for her state's department of aging and adult services. Her specialization is gerontology. She is responsible for management oversight and evaluation of programs funded by the federal Older Americans Act. This includes all programs for older and disabled adults such as pension programs, educational programs, and aid to the blind, and adult protection. Deb notes that, "Programs like these are becoming more and more important as our population ages. This is happening two ways. More people are making it to old age and those who have reached old age are living longer. Since most of us will eventually become an older American these programs are in our own best interests."

Deb's preparation for her job included a B.A. and M.A. in sociology. Her M.A. certified her as a gerontologist (as with criminal justice, gerontology degrees have had their genesis in, and are often still found within sociology departments). As a part of her M.A. program Deb served a one-year internship where she worked in long-term care systems development. Her work there consisted mostly of writing proposals, reports, and presentations, and doing occasional presentations herself. As time passed it became evident that Deb could produce the written reports and presentations on "very short notice." This ability provided several important opportunities. First, she became involved in a wide variety of agency work. She was able to see how different parts of the organization functioned, and what their various objectives were. Second, by being involved with different parts of the organization she was building an impressive personal network. As she demonstrated her ability to respond to diverse challenges in timely fashion word about her work spread within the agency. Deb observed that, "These kinds of processes are at work in all organizations. If you realize this then you can work these processes to your advantage." Deb's advantage was that people who needed her skills sought her out. Prior to completion of her M.A. Deb's effective work and her network resulted in occasional consultive work. According to Deb, "I earned between $500 and $1000 a month, outside of my practicum, in consulting work."

Deb's preparation for entree to state government agency work was her degree in sociology. She notes that, "Agency work is information work. As such, you have to know how to process or handle information. In addition, the information available often comes in a variety of forms. If the information is to be productive you have to be able to synthesize and condense it. You have to be able to see connections and know to look for information that is missing. Just as important, you must to know when you need information, and how to get information. All of these are fundamental sociological skills." Added to these are methodological specifics such as an ability to use SPSS (Statistical Package for the Social Science) on the computer, understanding what statistical numbers mean, and being able to construct data collection tools. According to Deb, "Sociology appears to be more balanced than some other disciplines. Others tend to have more narrow objectives. The result is that the sociologically prepared researcher is more likely to `see' the big picture of some project. This perspective is essential."

In addition to the specialized skills there is a natural connection between the sociologist as an organizational member and as a scholar of organizational behavior. This helps keep the sociologist, as a member of the organization, from becoming too narrowly focused. It also means that the sociologist can employ organizational skills which have long been a part of sociological scholarship. Deb commented in this regard that she "balances her identity as a sociologist and gerontologist. In some circles the research strengths of being a sociologist give me organizational authority, while at other times, especially in presentations, the title of gerontologist is most important. I also have to be careful to not offend people with a title. There is a bias, particularly among long-time employees, against those who are `college trained'."

When asked to describe a typical day Deb used the term "eclectic." There is no set pattern. She said, "Even when I have specific plans I simply have to expect that things will change. I am constantly switching gears, quickly and completely. This is simply a function of multiple tasks." Lately these tasks have been concentrated on acquisition and distribution of funding for the various agency programs. These would include writing grants, developing RFP's (requests for proposals: grant application forms for other agencies seeking money from Deb's agency), choosing grant evaluation teams, developing contracts for successful grantees, and training grantees. This is in addition to other necessary intra- and inter-organizational relations. The real need, according to Deb, is adaptability to change. Deb's agency has continued to accept interns, as she once was. However, Deb says that "Student interns have often been disappointing. They need to be self-starters. They must show initiative. They need to be able to deal with ambiguity. They must accept change. Actually they must anticipate change."

Now, after ten years Deb is pursuing an additional degree in sociology, her Ph.D. The need is to stay current. She recognizes that anticipating change applies to her as well as to intern students. Since 1984 Sue's salary has kept pace and has given her the freedom to pursue her doctorate; she now earns approximately $52,000 a year. When asked about her future, Deb said that she "expects more twists and terms," but she knows she "is prepared to make whatever adjustments are necessary."

When asked if she would recommend sociology to students making up their minds about a major, Deb said, "Absolutely!"

NOTE:

For more information important to this career see the following chapters in Sociology: A Down to Earth Approach, by James M. Henslin:

      Chapter 5 How Sociologists Do Research
      Chapter 7 Bureaucracy and Formal Organizations
      Chapter 13 Inequalities of Age
      Chapter 15 Politics: Power and Authority

13.

SOCIOLOGY AND CAREERS
IN CONSULTING-EDUCATION

Rod Fisher started his undergraduate education in a community college. Twenty-five years later we find Rod still in a community college, though with a far different perspective on sociology. As an undergraduate Rod admits that he "didn't pay much attention to sociology at first." However, he eventually found the "issues" addressed in sociology classes most interesting, and decided to pursue a major in the field. This interest persisted and developed as Rod eventually earned his M.A. and Ph.D. degrees. While he had developed advanced technical skills in methods and statistics Rod characterized his education as primarily formal. "There was no real emphasis in any of my degree programs on applied sociology."

For a person with advanced degrees but no real applied focus the options are not very broad. In Rod's case he found himself back in school, only this time as a professor in a community college. From Rod's point of view the community college presented a number of challenges. One challenge was competition for students. Four-year schools were perceived as having more quality and more opportunity. In this environment community colleges were not seen as places where the best students attended. Nor were they seen as a place of much scholarship. But to Rod these perceptions were challenges, not barriers. And, as challenges he sought ways around, over, or through them. To Rod the faculty and students of the college were a valuable resource. "These people were qualified and capable in a lot of different ways. What we needed to do was exercise and develop those capabilities."

The late 1970's brought together a number of circumstances which Rod saw as opportunities to make use of those capabilities he believed existed within those around him. Society was in the midst of many significant changes, racial and ethnic, urban and suburban, gender and age, economic, etc. People were experiencing changes in these and other areas of their lives, but not really understanding how to respond or relate. Unfortunately, experience itself is not necessarily sufficient for developing a meaningful response. Among other things, rapid change brings with it gaps in our information bases. According to Rod, "Information is what was needed, and the information had to be relevant. It had to pertain to local issues." In this context Rod and three colleagues, one from sociology, one from history, and another from speech and communications, pooled their resources and formed the Local Issues Research Institute (LIRI).

Formed in conjunction with the community college, LIRI engaged in a process of systematically studying community issues such as patterns of tourism in the area, women's concerns, quality of life for the elderly, and the local hospital's public image. In these initial studies Rod was able to establish a track record of quality research. In addition, LIRI was able to demonstrate how that well-produced information could have an impact. In the case of tourism it is important to know exactly where tourists go and why, how much money they spend, and what they think about their experiences. Based on such data a formal approach to tourism promotion could be produced. Or, steps could be taken to improve public perceptions of a local hospital and thereby influence the level of local health care delivery. According to Rod, the lesson here was and still is, "that good information is in demand and can be used to make a difference."

Early successes in local research led to other opportunities. One was research into the perceived quality of government services. Another focused on the future of local economic development. In one study nearly 200 CEO's were surveyed in face-to face interviews. Such data can help create a community atmosphere whereby economic development is enhanced. For example, this can occur by way of the Chamber of Commerce's communication of that CEO data to businesses and people considering moving to the area. The absence of such data would not necessarily prevent these moves, but these moves are not as likely without such data. In another instance LIRI was able to help police uncover local crime patterns. According to Rod, "In response to a series of local gas station murders, LIRI was able to do data analyses which accurately profiled where this crime was likely to occur. Contrary to most assumptions, these crimes were not occurring in the most isolated stations, but were occurring in convenience stores at or near closing time." Research like this helped local authorities better allocate scarce resources for both protection and apprehensions.

From the point of view of Rod's students the work of LIRI was an especially valuable opportunity. In LIRI projects Rod's students participated in all aspects of the research. They helped define problems, create models for data collection, administer the models, process data, and generate analyses, conclusions, and recommendations. For all this students received at least two valuable benefits. One, they graduated with concrete, applicable skills, and the experience necessary to make the essential connections between the discipline and the world outside of class. Two, the students were paid for their work! The result of this is that Rod's students have done more than learn sociology. They have become proactive within the discipline. They have been empowered through their discipline, to effectively "read" their environment, and themselves, and then choose a meaningful course of action.

Now that LIRI has been firmly established within his college, Rod has gone into private consulting. His focus is still local, but his array of services has expanded. He now competes for evaluation contracts, and consults in strategic planning and organizational development. According to Rod what is most important is his ability to "see the world" in unique ways. One problem with the common sense of clients is that it is based on assumptions which necessarily limit the client's perspective. This perspective is typically narrower and more individualistic than that offered by sociologists. In any consultation which involves change a broad perspective is essential if it is to be successful.

Rod's success in consultative work translates well in financial terms. For training workshops, such as he has done for the Federal Aviation Administration, he can earn up to $3,000 for two days of instruction. In other work Rod earns $65-$70 per hour. This includes work such as interviews, research design, data collection and analyses, and recommendation reports. Rod is clear in stating that the opportunities in this type of work are "diverse and expanding; good money can be made for good work."

Even though Rod's private work is expanding he has chosen to stay in education where he earns between $30,000 and $40,000 annually. His passion is still for students and he offers this advice. "Sociology is a core-skills discipline. Therefore, it is applicable in a variety of work settings." These skills also prepare you for advanced degrees in a variety of other disciplines. What is required is an aggressive posture on the part of the discipline. "We must not, as a discipline, wait for the world to come to us, we must be aggressive in telling our story." And that story, in Rod's experience is that, if well done, sociology has a real contribution to make.

NOTE:

For more information important to this career see the following chapters in Sociology: A Down to Earth Approach, by James M. Henslin:

Chapter 5 How Sociologists Do Research
Chapter 17 Education: Transferring Knowledge and Skills
Chapter 20 Population and Urbanization
Chapter 22 Social Change

14.

SOCIOLOGY AND CAREERS
IN CITY MANAGEMENT

Don Kratzer is the Director of the Department of Development for a mid-sized city, which is part of a major metropolitan area in the Midwest. While Don has been employed by this city in economic development work for 20 years, he is quick to point out that, "There have been big changes both in what I do and in the nature of economic development. You have to be able to change and adapt. If not, then the system can be quite unforgiving."

In 1974 Don began working for the City Planning Department. Interestingly, his degree background was an M.A. in nuclear engineering and physics. He had a natural facility with people, but no real training or education to prepare him for addressing the issues and problems of urban America. Nonetheless, when the Planning Department created an Economic Development Division Don was asked to head it up. Said Don, "It seemed that others felt I had administrative ability. I worked well with others. This, more than my knowledge of urban or economic issues, is why I was put in charge. It also helped that I had an advanced degree, even though it was in an unrelated field." The fact that he had a degree more or less added legitimacy to the appointment.

But, Don's academic degree provided more than minimal legitimacy. It also gave him experience in learning, and in learning how to learn. In an environment of change such a skill is essential. As Don noted, "We had to learn the business of economic development from the ground up." This is where Don's encounter with sociology begins. In the early 1980's Don began taking undergraduate and graduate courses in sociology, and eventually enrolled in a graduate Ph.D. program. According to Don, "I went into sociology at first simply to develop some job mobility. But as I took more courses in sociology I began to see the discipline as a way of better understanding the bigger picture of urban America. It has given me a handle on my own community, and has facilitated my interest in making a difference in my community."

As the Director of Economic Development Don is responsible for a wide array of functions. These include, but are not limited to community development, economic development, planning and zoning, building inspection, code enforcement, and maintenance of existing property. In carrying out these responsibilities Don oversees a staff of 65 employees. Management of this department requires all the insights organizational sociology can provide. According to Don, "Informal authority is often stronger than formal authority." And, the idea of "informal authority" is peculiarly sociological. As Don sees it, "Informal authority is a product of 20 years of experience, and most importantly, networking. You need to know and be known by the right people. This is just the way things get done. If you look at the work in narrow business terms then relatively little will get done. Sociologically one must be quite `open-systems' in approach. This is a real contributor of sociological theory to surviving in organizations."

Inter-departmental and inter-governmental relations are but one aspect of Don's job. When asked, Don divided his work into three parts. One-third of his time is spent administering his department. One-third is spent on large-scale development projects. And, one-third of his time is spent in direct contact with community and neighborhood groups dealing with local issues. Community relations is paramount because without grass-roots participation the objectives of urban development will not happen. "The citizens must embrace the problems as well as the solutions. Also, given that development is so politically connected citizens must be informed so that they can act politically."

One specific aspect of information for citizens is helping them see personal/neighborhood issues in community/structural perspective. What sociological theory does, notes Don, "is to help adequately `frame' the issue at hand so that we can actually address it." The problem is that so many times people's actions are unrelated to their objectives. The reason is that they cannot clearly "see" how they and their actions fit into the larger picture. Don's job is to help channel the desire for action into functional action, into effective goal accomplishing action.

To perform his work effectively Don suggests that basic sociological skills and insights are necessary. Data are always being collected through surveys, interviews and other forms of observation. And, these data must be processed so that it is meaningful and ultimately useful. In dealing with the public Don often has to practice the qualitative method of empathy. "I must put my feet in their shoes." By seeing issues from their point of view one can better respond to those issues. In so doing, Don and his staff are able to address one of the more important realities of modern urban centers, cultural diversity. Working well in a culturally diverse city requires great flexibility and adaptability. Says Don, "You have to find the most effective way to communicate your message regardless of your audience." Unfortunately failure is a reality, at least part of the time. "You must be able to handle frustration in this job. This means you simply have to find another solution. The problems of urban life have been 200 years in the making so solutions are not likely to be easily found or easily implemented. But this is our challenge, and sociology is excellent preparation for the task."

There is a tendency, however, for students trained in sociology not to be prepared for the "hard edge" of non-academic work. While sociology provides a "great critique" on society "we must translate that critique into real world action." Therefore, according to Don, "I have to be able to condense the theoretic framing process into a one-page policy statement for departmental action. Most academic sociologists simply cannot do this. By the time many academics could get around to a position on some issue, the issue itself may have changed. We need real-time solutions to real-time problems. But, if you can make the adjustment, then the urban scene provides a great opportunity for the discipline."

Given that cities will continue being a part of our society, the discipline of sociology will continue to have a field of contribution. Don sees many important opportunities for those students of sociology who can make the transition to non-academic settings. Entry level positions as mid-level managers require research and project management skills. This level of work now pays annual salaries of $30,000 - $40,000. With the Ph.D. now in hand Don, as a department director, earns approximately $60,000 - $65,000. "Yes, a living can be made," according to Don, "but perhaps more importantly, I believe I can make a difference in my community."

NOTE:

For more information important to this career see the following chapters in Sociology: A Down to Earth Approach, by James M. Henslin:

15.

SOCIOLOGY AND CAREERS
IN EVALUATION RESEARCH

Mike Howard is a senior program evaluator for a major private research and consulting company. Ninety percent of the company's work is connected to state and federal contracts. These contracts typically call for policy studies or program evaluation research. In policy studies the objective is to develop new or redevelop existing policies in accordance with organizational missions. These policies are then submitted as recommendations for adoption and/or revision by the contracting organization. In program evaluation the objective is to determine how well an existing program is meeting its goals. This is important for development of the program or termination of programs which are not successful. Over 300 employees of this company are involved in such work in three major offices across the country.

Mike earned B.A., M.A., and Ph.D. degrees in sociology, but his path was not exactly direct. When asked about his B.A. Mike said, "I had no specific goals, although I thought there might be some future in government. My parents were in government and I had some idea how things worked and how sociology might fit." Early on Mike knew he would pursue a Ph.D. but just when, where, and how was an open question. Initially he took a series of jobs in both teaching and social work. In one way this served to focus his attention and interests in the area of social welfare. Mike also began to see a need for concrete applications of his discipline to the problems he was studying.

After completing his doctorate Mike continued teaching but also began looking for other opportunities. He found some in contract assessment and evaluation work on a part-time basis. His first work in this area was in response to an ad in the newspaper for a person with a background in welfare policy and research. The job offered both full and part time consulting opportunities and, according to Mike, "higher salary scales than I could expect to achieve in teaching."

The contract was for a federal study of how states administer welfare and Medicaid programs. The issue was the use, by states, of data on welfare/Medicaid eligibility error rates. The potential problem is that people who are not eligible may somehow be defined as eligible. Because of errors in determining eligibility, money budgeted for these programs is not always well spent. The task is to minimize these errors. The only way to do so is research the processes by which eligibility is determined. The method of research was telephone interviews. Several different interview schedules were used so as to not artificially produce patterned results. Mike noted that, "While I was interviewing people from the same kinds of agencies it became very evident that I was dealing with different types of local organizations, different perspectives on the work being done and different ideas about the research I was conducting." Methodologically, Mike conducted content analyses, a quantitative process, to determine common denominators among similar, yet different agencies, so as to produce a uniform report. At stake was the appropriate distribution of thousands, or perhaps even millions of dollars per agency. This is important work.

After completing the study on eligibility error rates Mike decided to leave teaching and go to work full time for the same company. The following is one of the projects Mike has been working on. It is an evaluation of the implementation of substance abuse prevention programs. Funding for the study has come from the Center for Substance Abuse Prevention (CSAP). The study will take three years to complete. The CSAP has already funded 130 substance abuse prevention demonstration programs targeting youth. It is Mike's job to evaluate these programs for the purpose of developing an overall strategy for fighting substance abuse.

The tasks and issues confronting Jack are numerous and complex. The insights and skills of the sociologist are at a premium. These include, but are by no means limited to, defining the issues and problems faced by such programs, selecting data collection techniques, selecting a sample of 60 from 130 projects across the U.S., operationalizing significant variables, writing case study reports, writing cross-site reports (comparing sites), and leading site visits for data collection. In addition there are special topics such as program services to targeted populations based on gender and/or ethnicity. To get an idea of the size of the study Mike suggests looking at the final report. "There will be sixty individual program reports, each averaging forty pages. While the writing keeps you busy, it is the logistics of actually producing the program reports that really test you." An additional challenge, according to Mike, is "that the individual programs are so diverse and new that there is not much in common among them and little is known ahead of time about how they were working. This calls for a very flexible methodology so we can adjust as we go along."

To all of the research issues just mentioned you must also add, according to Mike, the "two worlds of the project manager." One of these is the research company's point of view. Here the project manager must deal with the composition of site visit teams, as well as internal project staff. Mike notes that, "The company is concerned with matters of personnel and the issues of task; what must be done and who will do it? But, you are working for a client (for example, CSAP) and they have their own interests and needs." In contracts with government there is the project officer for the government who is interested in task and a deliverable project. Then there is the government contract officer who is interested in the project budget variables and whether the work actually satisfies the contract. These people, and other related supervisors from the client perspective wield a great deal of influence. "Sometimes," according to Mike, "there is difficulty in attempting to please the client while staying within the parameters of the contract. This can be a very delicate balancing act." Then, in a multi-year contract there is always the potential for personnel turnover. This can easily upset the balance you have worked so hard to achieve. Mike adds that, "Managing a project like this is really a matter of managing all the various relationships. Because of this you must always be on top of things. If not, you can lose control quite easily."

Mike's job, as can be seen, is a varied mix of tasks, relationships and perspectives. His work is not simply researching a question, but managing the intricacies of organizational life. For example, all contracts have their beginning in a proposal. The client publishes an RFP--request for proposals--which outlines the project the client envisions. According to Mike, "It is important to anticipate RFP's, because once they are published the contracting company cannot have discussions with clients (if the client is the government). If you already have a good client relationship then you can find out what is going to happen before it happens. This way you can have all the discussions you want." This suggests the influence of structures outside what may be defined as official. "By and large," according to Mike, "a lot of what we do is informal rather than formal. Your personal network is a very valuable resource. It does matter who you know and by whom you are known."

When asked to connect his studies in sociology to his work as a researcher Mike suggested that, "There is very little that I do which is not informed by sociology." Organizational theory and management have obvious connections. "You are constantly applying your knowledge of how organizations function just to stay on top of your job. For example, the difference between formal/and informal is readily clear to the sociologist trained in organizational behavior. Such an understanding, however, is not a part of some other disciplines." General theory is also quite valuable. Mike notes that, "You are always dealing with people as they try to relate to each other. This is the essence of sociology and theory is an important tool in understanding, or framing some situation." So often people get caught up in the local or immediate issues. Sociological theory helps one see the larger and longer range picture. According to Mike, "Without this perspective there is no viable way to really evaluate a program."

In addition to theory, methodological skill is always in demand. According to Mike, "Methodological abilities are extremely important. But beyond competence, you must be creative. No two situations will be just alike." A part of methods is statistics, and in this regard Mike advises that, "You have to know how to crunch the numbers. I am always doing this to some extent." Finally according to Mike, "None of the skills will mean much if you cannot communicate. You have to be able to write all types of things from reports, to summaries, to letters, memos, etc. You will also have to make oral presentations, as well as simply speak clearly in your work." The computer is always a part of the work, so computer literacy is a must. According to Mike, "Our employees must be able to use software such as Word Perfect, Lotus, D-Base, and SPSS-PC." Without this capability it is not possible to do the job.

It is the case, however, that sociology is a discipline which does prepare the student for the above challenges. "The critical perspective of sociology sharpens the mind," according to Mike, and this promotes the kinds of competence and skills necessary. Mike does suggest that, "students actively seek internships or volunteer positions which challenge them to immediately begin applying the classroom to the real world. It's also quite good on a resume." Regardless of your preparation, Mike clearly points out that what ultimately matters most is, "Can you do the job? People don't care what your degree is as long as you are productive. It's just that sociology can give you a real advantage over other disciplines."

Finally, what about making a living? In Mike's company entry-level positions will pay $30,000 - $45,000 depending on skills, capabilities, experience and education. Senior staff, like Mike, will earn from $50,000 to $100,000. Top level vice presidents will earn from $90,000 - $120,000. Presidents will earn from $150,000 to $175,000. "But the bottom line is, can you do the job? If you can, you will make a good living."

NOTE:

For more information important to this career see the following chapters in Sociology: A Down to Earth Approach, by James M. Henslin:

Chapter 5 How Sociologists Do Research
Chapter 7 Bureaucracy and Formal Organizations
Chapter 15 Politics: Power and Authority

16.

SOCIOLOGY AND CAREERS
IN LAW

Jeff Franklin presently serves as executive director of a state health care policy commission. The commission is comprised of representatives from across the health care industry including, but not limited to, doctors, hospital administrators, insurance executives, special health interest lobbyists, etc. Their job is to meet and negotiate the future of their state's health care system. As executive director it is Jeff's job to see to it that those people fulfill their mission.

He does this primarily in three ways. One, he is to maintain the "visionary perspective." According to Jeff, "While these people are all experts in some area of health care they often are focused on immediate problems and issues. I have to keep them thinking about what our health care system should be like in ten years." Two, Jeff is an organizational manager. As such, "I oversee a staff of researchers, analysts, writers, etc. The primary need is for valid information and clear communications, and the commission is responsible for this." Jeff must see to it that the organization operates effectively and efficiently. Three, Jeff maintains a complex set of relations, with himself at the center, among the health care industry, clients of health care industry, the legislature, and governor, and other special interests including average citizens. Mike suggests that, "This is my real job, serving as a hub, linking all these people together." In health care Jeff's position is one of significant influence. Most of the commissions's policy statements have been enacted into law in one of the most progressive health care reform states in the country. More details of his work will follow, but first we will examine how Jeff came to this position.

In the mid-1970's Jeff graduated from a small Christian Liberal Arts College with a degree in sociology. According to Jeff, "As important as my degree in sociology was the college's focus and insistence on the development of values. The world is so full of people who simply don't care about others and are there only for themselves. Basic values must be addressed and developed if one is to make a positive contribution." It is this combination of degree and value commitment which led Jeff to social service work. "My first real job was as a financial case worker for a large county/metropolitan area social service system." In this capacity Jeff became familiar with a wide array of family services, agencies, and needs. The technical work was determining eligibility for financial assistance. However, according to Jeff, "The issues were always more complex than money. I had to determine what the real underlying needs were and then seek ways to match services with those needs."

The connections between this work and Jeff's degree are many. Jeff notes that, "It is surprising to most people just how important a proper perspective is for solving a problem." What many may see as an "attitude" may actually be behavior generated by a complex set of environmental variables. However, according to Jeff, "This does not mean that individuals are without responsibility." But it does mean that "solutions to problems may be a matter of putting together the right combination of external services."   This perspective is one which embraces the concept of community. It sees the individual as part of a larger complex of relations. For this, according to Jeff, "sociology is a natural and productive discipline." Jeff stayed in this line of work for about eight years, starting in the late seventies at a salary of around $18,000. By the mid eighties he had worked his way through the system and was earning approximately $25,000.

As Jeff's career developed within the social service system he took on various jobs. Toward the end of his time as a direct provider of social services Jeff began working in crisis intervention. His work was on weekends and nights, a time when people often confront their problems of family and life. His job was to see to it that an appropriate array of social services were brought to bear on whatever a client defined as a crisis. According to Jeff, "Sometimes this meant helping people see that what they thought was a major crisis was actually a small problem which they could handle themselves. For others it meant emergency action. We dealt with everything from child abuse to illness to the aftereffects of a house fire." In Jeff's opinion, "The crisis intervention work really was quite satisfying. In many ways you could actually see the results of your efforts to help people in need. But there was a downside. My efforts were limited to case by case help. There were always more cases. My idea was that if I could exert influence at the county or state administrative level then perhaps I could do more than deal with cases after crises had already occurred."

Jeff's solution was to take advantage of his schedule, which freed his days, to enter law school. Upon graduation Jeff took a job with the legislative research staff of his state's senate. His special area of research was human services. According to Jeff, his work was always varied, yet went something like the following. A senator would come to the research staff and identify some particular problem or issues he/she wanted to address with legislation. Jeff's job was to ultimately draft that legislation; to convert the issue into law. This required a number of skills which were particularly sociological in nature. As Jeff suggests, "My law degree got me into this job, but the work could be characterized as basic sociology." Much like his work in the social services system Jeff had to help his client, in this case a legislator, define clearly the issue/problem at hand. Then it was a matter of gathering information relevant to that definition. Sometimes this meant doing basic research, at other times it meant requesting it from other sources.

In this regard Jeff notes that, "Being able to read and understand research is such an important skill." When people would present data Jeff was able to ascertain, better than most, its validity. For example, when reviewing survey reports Jeff would be able to discern between well and poorly written questions. Therefore, while data may indicate a particular course of action, if those data were the result of poor data collection then the course of action should be questioned. Jeff used these skills over and over again as legislative questions were being framed.

Jeff was also in a position to exercise theoretic interpretation. Once an issue was defined it was in need of a solution. The creation of a solution required a clear understanding of the social dynamics involved. A theoretic perspective suggests places to look for problem definition, and therefore avenues of altering the situation so that a solution could be produced. In collaboration with the senator Jeff then wrote the legislation. But this was not the conclusion of his work. He then needed to help "explain" the legislation to others. Others included state agencies, potential clients, the public, and other law-makers. Jeff's intimate knowledge of the issue, both theoretically and methodologically, put him in a critical position for communication.

Every year it was something different in legislative research. For ten years Jeff worked on human services and social issues as diverse as welfare reform, gender equity, and most recently, health care reform. The sociological contributions were many and went well beyond methodology. As Jeff once suggested, "Legislation is like a large competition with many participants. Information is the key and common ingredient. With the right information you can create, control and direct policy. You see, the legislature is not itself out in the field figuring out how the world is working. Yet they have the power to set policy which influences how the world does work." This makes the work of information handlers all that more significant. The whole process must be carefully managed. Meanings must be well-constructed, communications clear, and alliances vigorously pursued. For this a clear understanding of organizations and networks, as well as individuals is absolutely necessary. According to Jeff, "This is an intensely interactional process. An understanding of interaction is therefore most important." In fact, there is little or nothing about this work which is not informed by sociology. During this time Jeff was earning a salary ranging from the low $30,000's to the mid $40,000's.

As a result of his work in the legislature Jeff came to be known for a number of traits. He is known as being value- driven and a person of integrity. He was also well known for his skills in information production and management. His network extended throughout state government and outside state government. That brings us to the present and his work with the commission, for which he earns approximately $60,000 annually. Jeff believes that he has the opportunity for more significant input. In one sense Jeff sees himself as an average citizen exercising whatever influence he can wield. He has seen it before, and studies it. It is an ongoing part of our society, one with which Jeff intends to stay involved. Further, as Jeff's career has developed so far, he fully expects it to continue developing.

This expectation of continuing career development is a point of advice which Jeff offers to current students. Research and communication skills are an obvious must. But perspective is as important, especially perspective recognizing the significance of values. This is not work for those whose values are uncertain. Add to this assertiveness and aggressiveness. Jeff urges a proactive pursuit of all options. This begins in school where the broad, multifaced education is recommended According to Jeff, "My career has been highly rewarding at each stage, and I have high expectations for the future. There is still a lot of work to be done. There always will be. Those who are prepared will be the ones to make a difference."

NOTE:

For more information important to this career see the following chapters in Sociology: A Down to Earth Approach, by James M. Henslin:

17.

SOCIOLOGY AND CAREERS
IN CHILD WELFARE

Ellen Harrington was determined to pursue a degree which would prepare her "to help people. Sociology gave me the perspective I needed, as well as some specific tools." By perspective Ellen means, the ability to see a problem or some situation in a productive or perhaps unique way. For example, Ellen suggests that, "A legal perspective might define a family as those related by blood and/or marriage and who also reside at the same address. A sociological perspective might help one see that a common name and address does not necessarily mean functional family relations. Many people can identify with being close to someone in proximity, but not close as a friend. In the case of a family the sociologist would look at actual relationships and the nature of those relationships in determining how to deal with a collection of people as a family."

According to Ellen there is another way in which sociology provides perspective, and this is found in the discipline's method. The focus on research in sociology means that new data are always being produced. Research skills possessed by individual sociologists allows one to produce their own data whenever current data are insufficient. As a result, perspective is something that is dynamic. It is always developing. But this only makes sense, according to Ellen, "because the nature of human issues continues to evolve. Ten years ago we really weren't hearing anything about AIDS. Before AIDS it was crack babies. Before that it was issues of recreational drug use and the disintegration of traditional families. Now we are talking about blended families and cultural diversity." The lesson to be learned is, if one's perspective is static then they will become less and less effective as circumstances change.

After earning her B.A. Ellen went directly to graduate school and earned her Masters in Social Work (MSW) degree. An increasingly popular degree, MSW programs can be entered from a variety of undergraduate degrees including sociology, psychology, undergraduate social work, and even business and education. Several things make the MSW popular, foremost among them being flexibility. "There are so many directions that a person can go with an MSW," according to Ellen. In her case she went to work for an agency to which she had been introduced by her undergraduate advisor. With her MSW in hand Venessa entered the work force as a principal case worker doing investigations. This was the top entry level position in her organization, and gave her significant responsibilities. One year later Ellen was promoted to Social Services Specialist II, a licensed position, and one recognized with the title of Master Social Worker.

Ellen's responsibilities were significant and varied. She investigated allegations of child abuse and neglect. Specifically she investigated child sexual abuse. Her work would begin with a case of potential abuse being reported to her agency. These reports could come from neighbors, teachers, doctors, and even family members. In coordination with the local police, and according to a special protocol, Ellen would begin investigating by interviewing victims. According to Ellen, "The difficulty here is determining what has really happened versus what people believe or perceive has happened. It is also difficult to get people to trust you, as the investigator, and therefore provide the information you need. In many ways this is just basic sociological research."

Subsequent to an investigation which determined that abuse had occurred Ellen then worked with the district attorney in superior court in prosecution of the case. According to Ellen, "What was especially important here was consulting with the authorities so that they fully and clearly understood the case. The law may be 'black and white' but cases of actual abuse are usually 'gray.' In sociological terms you are constructing realities about what occurred in ways that people can respond."

In addition to her duties as investigator Ellen was involved in a number of other projects. Her skills in research and her ability to communicate the nuances of her work made her a widely recognized expert in the community. She conducted training seminars for the police department on recognizing the indicators of abuse. She participated in U.S. Department of Justice research on the handling of domestic violence cases by police. And, she advised the courts on the benefits of prison verses intervention in prosecuting a case. She also consulted other agencies which had reason to come in contact with children and families. The important career point here is, Ellen's career developed well beyond the standard parameters of her job. Her discipline gave her the perspective to see more opportunities for her work than a simple job description might lead one to believe.

One way Ellen's career developed was to change careers. After about eight years Ellen returned to school and eventually earned the Ph.D. in social work. But instead of advancing within the field of social work, Ellen moved into higher education. Now she is preparing students for careers in social work. As usual, however, Ellen does more than simply teach. She has promoted learning opportunities for students outside the classroom and has served the community generally. For example, when the local school district was sponsoring a youth leadership development conference Ellen was asked to present a seminar on gangs. Rather than lecturing, Ellen had her juvenile delinquency class prepare and present skits and other role playing performances to teach young people about gangs. In addition to all this Ellen is taking on yet a new challenge. In her mid 30's and after earning her Ph.D., Ellen is learning a second language, Spanish. Her reasoning is, "With the United States being one of this worlds largest

Spanish speaking countries, and with that population being one of the fastest growing in the U.S., it just seemed like I ought to be prepared. Besides, when my students complain about having to take Spanish I can say that I'm in their with them." To this end Ellen even engaged in an immersion program in the Dominican Republic. Ellen advises, "The learning never stops."

Financially, social work does not necessarily mean low pay. According to Ellen, "You will not make a lot of money, but you can be comfortable." For large urban areas Ellen reports the following type of pay scale. Entry level with a B.A. starts at $20,000 - $25,000. First year MSW's can earn at about $30,000. Ph.D.'s can make $40,000 - $50,000. In addition the flexibility of the degree allows those who are motivated to become entrepreneurial and set up clinics or go into private counseling. In this case the earnings potential is great; from $50 to $150 per hour, depending on locale, population, and kind of service offered.

Two others, Todd and Tracie Abbott, are just embarking on their careers. Todd was an undergraduate psychology major and Tracie majored in sociology. Their interests tended towards the human services, but both realized that additional education would be necessary. There was also a complicating factor. Todd was a year ahead in college and he and Tracie were intent on getting married soon. Tracie's parents were somewhat concerned about educational expenses and job prospects. The solution was an accelerated program for Tracie whereby she was admitted into a graduate MSW program after her junior year in college. This effectively caught her up with Todd who was also entering the same MSW program. Two years later they are both graduates with MSW's in hand and, significantly, jobs. Tracie is a clinical therapist focusing on children and Todd is a clinical outpatient therapist focusing on adults. Located in a small town Todd and Tracie find that there is still tremendous need for their services. As far as their parents are concerned, the payback for education has already begun. Both Todd and Tracie have entry level salaries of $25,000, for a combined income of $50,000. "We're not sure just exactly what to expect," say Todd and Tracie, "but we know we are prepared. It's just a matter of using the knowledge we have and being willing to look for and take advantage of the opportunities. It's exciting."

NOTE:

For more information important to this career see the following chapters in Sociology: A Down to Earth Approach, by James M. Henslin:

Chapter 3 Socialization
Chapter 8 Deviance and Social Control
Chapter 10 Social Class in American Society
Chapter 16 The Family: Our Introduction to Society

18.

SOCIOLOGY AND CAREERS
IN GERONTOLOGY

By her own account, Arlene Mollett's career in sociology began while "sitting on the curb." Arlene's undergraduate degree was in education and she had been teaching in the public school system. For some time Arlene had been interested in law school and decided to go forward with an application. However, she found that she was late for that year's entrance exam and would have to wait another year. On the advice of friends she sought to keep her study skills sharp by pursuing an M.A. in education. However, according to Arlene, "When I went to the education office for advice on the M.A. program I found that there really wasn't anyone around who could help me. I needed to do something because time was short so I decided to look at other programs. But I found the same thing, no one was around who could help me." It was at this time that Arlene found herself sitting on the curb, pondering what to do next. While there a former professor of Arlene's, a professor of sociology, happened by and stopped to chat. When hearing her story he suggested that she pursue sociology. Arlene took the advice and eventually earned her M.A. in a program which was largely academic in emphasis.

After earning her M.A. Arlene left public school teaching and took a college teaching position. The courses she taught were rather straightforward academic sociology. She had acquired skills and perspectives, but did not see the these as potential resources. Eventually, because of university rules for faculty development Arlene needed to move on to the next degree, the Ph.D. While the selection of sociology as the discipline for the Ph.D. was not as serendipitous as with the M.A., her choice of graduate school and specialization bore similar markings. Her choice of school did include quality considerations, but she was as motivated by family concerns as well. She needed to stay within a reasonable distance of extended family. Her eventual choice of gerontology as her primary specialty had less apparent reason. According to Arlene, "My advisor suggested that I take a course in gerontology because all the other good classes were full."

Amazingly enough, that beginning, "on the curb," has mushroomed over the next dozen years in to a career that has influenced national policy regarding older Americans and has resulted in the allocations of millions of dollars in public and private resources. When asked about these rather haphazard beginnings to a highly successful career Arlene offers the following perspective. "My career in sociology/gerontology certainly wasn't planned. I look at it as a series of `differential opportunities!' But more importantly I've learned that if you are good at what you are doing, things will work out. This is not luck however, it is intentional. What it takes is, doing your homework, being enthusiastic, being positive, accepting no substitute for hard work, not being afraid to say `I don't know', and quickly adding, `but I will find out', accepting an element of risk, and focusing on the fun and enjoyment of what you do. When it is no longer fun, do something else."

Arlene's "philosophy of life" does, however, have its concrete edges. After completing her Ph.D. she returned to college teaching and took on the directorship of her university's gerontology institute. She also chaired the university's master's program in gerontology. Under her leadership the program can now boast of a 98% placement rate for graduates! In the Institute Arlene oversees a program of contract research for, and services to, agencies and organizations servicing the elderly. In the year past her institute did business totaling nearly $500,000. Add to this Arlene's lecture circuit work and consulting and you have a most high-profile career. In speaking fees alone Arlene earns in the neighborhood of $30,000 per year. In consulting she earns from $250 - $1000 per day. Nationally known speakers/consultants can earn $500 to $1500 per day. Arlene is in this league, but chooses to do part of her work as a service to those whom she serves, older Americans. The point is, when Arlene says, "do your homework," this is more than an admonition to work hard towards some ambiguous goal. It is a concrete course of action with definite objectives and quantifiable results. It should be remembered that Arlene does all this while maintaining a position as a full-time faculty member with an income in the $40,000-$50,000 range.

In fact, since that "curb" Arlene has developed three careers. She teaches, administers the institute, and speaks/consults. The following briefly reviews her work in these areas. In the institute she administers an organization designed to meet the needs of different types of elder-service agencies/organizations. This would include doing statistical analyses for county needs assessments regarding the lives of older people, conference management for organizations providing continuing education, technical reports, and training manuals. In her speaking/consulting Arlene works with agencies/organizations which service older Americans in a variety of ways. She will develop presentations and do training for elder service management, Alzheimer awareness, elder abuse, and interviewing skills. The significance of this is that in our country we are in a position of having to learn as we go along regarding older Americans. Each year we experience more and new relations with older Americans. How to deal effectively with this growing population is the challenge. Therefore, nearly all organizations, and certainly all communities and families will have to evaluate and improve the ways they have normally dealt with the elderly. Some have referred to the elderly as the population with the most economic growth potential. This means that there is great demand for elder services, and thus great demand for people proficient in the field, gerontologists. This is where her third career hooks in. As a professor she prepares students, a younger generation, to anticipate the needs of and provide necessary services for an older generation. Her placement rate of graduates attest to her success in this endeavor.

In terms of sociology, Arlene wants students to know that "no other discipline prepares them so broadly." Many disciplines prepare you well, but for only one type of work, or with one set of skills. In sociology you find not only a wide variety of sub-disciplines, but a perspective which promotes adaptability and learning. Arlene notes that, "You are always dealing with groups of people, whatever the issue, and this is basic sociology." In one sense, once you are in the discipline then all variables of life can be informed from the perspective of that discipline. Only if you escape people altogether could you possibly escape the parameters of sociology.

Arlene has blended her discipline and her philosophy of life into a multifaceted career. It is one which is always busy, but one which still meets the prerequisite of "fun and enjoyment." She advances the cause of older Americans by influencing the lives of younger Americans. She communicates and teaches others to perceive the world of the elderly in new ways. And her audience is as likely to be governors and senators as it is to be students and primary care givers. It is a long way from that "curb." But it is a way she would not exchange for another.

NOTE:
For more information important to this career see the following chapters in Sociology: A Down to Earth Approach, by James M. Henslin:

      Chapter 5 How Sociologists Do Research
      Chapter 13 Inequalities of Age
      Chapter 15 Politics: Power and Authority
      Chapter 16 The Family: Our Introduction to Society
      Chapter 17 Education: Transferring Knowledge and Skills

19.

SOCIOLOGY AND CAREERS
IN BUSINESS

Dave Blume and Bob Chase both earned undergraduate degrees in business. In addition, Dave and Bob also earned second degrees in sociology. According to Dave, "The competition in the business world can be very intense. You have to give potential employers a reason to select you over other candidates who have the same business degree that you do. Sociology, with its focus on groups, organizations, and human interaction is a natural compliment to business. And, it is a degree which is increasingly well-received in the business world." Bob adds, "There is so much that has changed in the way business is conducted that companies are looking for people who can be very flexible. People socialized in some of the older business patterns are just so inflexible that they cannot adjust. Sociology prepares you for understanding change and anticipating it. The degree is a real asset."

The important point is, conducting business requires well-managed human relationships. Two types of relationships are especially significant. The first is relations within the business organization itself. Inside any organization there are a complex array of roles. Imagine the relational adaptations required to manage interactions among engineers, secretaries, accountants, professionals, managers, blue-collar workers, CEO's, etc. Add to this the changing face of the organization itself. With hostile takeovers, mergers, downsizing, restructuring, and other changes in the business world, how easy is it to keep on top of essential business relations? Recently two major airlines have been financially salvaged by employee buy-outs. The employees are now the owners. How might this influence traditional management-labor relations? Complicating this is the manner in which we actually conduct these relations. According to Bob, "Much of the time we treat business relations as interpersonal relations; that is, relations among friends. The problem arises when a person's behavior is being determined by their official role and that role conflicts with the interpersonal role to which we have become accustomed. The sociological perspective allows me to see behind a person's actions and not take everything personally."

The second type of relationships important to business are those conducted with clients, or customers of the organization. According to Dave, "A lot of new people have culture shock when they begin working their first job. The problem, at least in sales, is that new sales people don't realize that there is an important difference between what they see as their product and what customers want. While I sell sports equipment my customers are mostly interested in service. If you can't put yourself in the shoes of your customers and see things from their perspective then you are going nowhere. In sociology you learn to dig behind surface appearances so you can see what is really motivating a person's behavior. The connection of this to sales is both straightforward and important." One thing which must be understood about modern customers, according to Bob, is that "Customer preferences frequently change. In banking what people seem to want is convenience. While some in banking understand this, many cling to old ideas which tend to put the bank first and the customer second. People want the bank 'to come to them' in the shape of longer hours, more locations, and fewer hassles in the bank itself. If you are not constantly researching customer preferences and perspectives then you will find yourself falling behind your competitors and losing your customers."

The important lesson so far is that without a good understanding of others, co-workers, superiors and subordinates, customers, and competitors, and how to relate to them, it is nearly impossible to succeed in business. In addition, sociology is a discipline which enhances a business person's ability to manage these relations. According to Dave, "The details of business are pretty easy to learn. What most students don't understand is that they must ultimately learn to read the interests of those who are important to them, and then figure out a way to satisfy those interests. In fact, if possible you need to know what a client, or your boss wants, even before they actually tell you. This means you must always be in a learning/researching mode. You are constantly observing and making notes on the patterns of these people. What sociology does for me is provide the tools and perspectives necessary to do this part of my work."

Since graduation Dave and Bob have taken thorough advantage of their education in both business and sociology. Of particular importance has been their success at recognizing, building, and accessing networks. Both took advantage of college-related networks to secure first positions. For example, Dave's college had a long-standing relationship with the CEO of a major sports management corporation. Each year the CEO would hire, at the recommendation of the college, a "personal assistant." Upon graduation Dave was recommended and hired for this position. According to Dave, "While the job really didn't pay very much in terms of money, it paid great dividends in expanding my networks. Unfortunately some who have filled this position just haven't understood this potential. In my opinion, my sociological perspective fostered the development of my own network. This was one of the repeated themes in my sociology courseware." According to Bob, "I would not have the job I how have had it not been for there being a network connection. The advantage was that my application was given more personal attention than others because I was from the same college as one of the bank officers. This alone did not get me the job. I had to take an exam and go through three interviews. But without something that made me stand out -- my place in a common network -- I doubt I would have been noticed. Some see this as an unfair advantage. I see it as the intelligent use of a resource available to anyone willing to work at it."

Since graduating from college five years ago Dave's career has mirrored national trends in the rate of job changes. As mentioned, Dave began his career as a personal assistant for the CEO of a major sports management corporation. Dave notes that, "I learned that this business was all about people skills. The gift that my boss had was to make any person feel as if they were most important to him. Even his letters have a very personal ring to them. Clients just feel comfortable with him." Success with some of the biggest names in professional sports attest to this particular strength.

Dave carefully observed his mentor's practices, including building his own network, and after his year of service was completed he was able to take a job in the sports equipment industry. He worked as a regional sales representative for a tennis equipment company. His responsibility was for developing a new region in terms of new accounts and increasing the business volume of existing accounts. In three years Dave was extremely successful in his work as he was several times named "national salesman of the month," and once was named "national salesman of the year."

Two characteristics were especially important for Dave's success. First, Dave had excellent customer relations. According to Dave, "So many sales reps simply go through the motions with clients. I make it a point to actually listen to what they say. Further I make literal notes on what they say. I learned this while working as a personal assistant. You just can't remember everything when you have so many things to remember." This practice served as a kind of market data for managing accounts. Second, Dave had to develop good intra-company contacts. Dave notes that, "The idea of a network applies not only to clients, but also to the company in which you work. This matched the idea of informal organization I studied in sociology." With the right organizational contacts Dave was then in a good position to service his clients in a timely fashion.

Because of Dave's success other sports equipment companies actively recruited him for their sales forces. One of them provided a complimentary line of products -- shoes and clothing. While his first company preferred he sold only their product they did not want to lose him and allowed him to carry the extra line. However, according to Dave, "I now had to learn a new organizational structure; one which was larger, more formal, and more bureaucratic. Networking in this company was more difficult because of the greater degree of division of labor. So, I had to work harder and be more creative." Again Dave achieved a good level of success as evidenced by yet other companies pursuing his services.

Now Dave works for one of the largest racket sport equipment companies in the world. In this case Dave made the move, leaving his other two companies, for two reasons. One, was offered a secure salaried position with excellent benefits. In his previous work his income was based solely on commissions. The other reason is that with his new position he now has worked in nearly all aspects of the racket sports industry. According to Dave, "I'm learning the last part of this business." Such a perspective speaks to Dave's long-range orientation. "I must be fully prepared for whatever the future brings. If there is one thing my combination of degrees taught me it is to expect change, and therefore be prepared for it."

By being prepared Dave has managed to be successful financially in a very competitive industry. In his last year working on commission, as an independent contractor for two companies, Dave earned $65,000 - $70,000. Today, in a salaried position, with benefits, a car, etc., his salary is approximately $50,000. Yet, as successful as he has been Dave is now considering a return to school. According to Dave, "I may have gone as far as I can without more education. I'm sure that in the next few years I'll be pursuing an MBA. I have to stay on top of industry trends. If I get too comfortable others will soon be passing me by."

Bob's career, still in its first year, is far less developed, but just as interesting sociologically. Bob is on the cutting edge of banking services in what is called, "supermarket banking." Because of consumer demands for convenience and service, banks have begun opening more branch locations which offer a complete set of bank services. For example, at Bob's branch you not only can cash a check, you can borrow money for a car or even refinance your mortgage. "The problem within the banking industry," according to Bob, "is that existing employees simply could not make the needed transformation to a more consumer-driven pattern of work. In fact, many people in traditional banking tended to see the bank as having priority over the customer, not the other way around."

Supermarket banking requires a more organizationally aggressive, but user friendly approach. It also has a much flatter, less departmentalized organizational structure. Bob notes that, "In banking it is not just a matter of making organizations flatter, these new branches are simply constructed without any real hierarchy. We work much more like a team where everybody knows everybody else's business. In a traditional bank you have very separate departments for each function." In terms of service, according to Bob, "The supermarket branches are more approachable. In a traditional bank setting the customer must be available during normal bank hours which often isn't very convenient. Then, for each service they need they have to go and wait in line in each department. At the branches the bank comes to the customer with longer hours and one stop service, meaning one bank employee is capable of servicing all needs." Obviously this type of banking is people intensive. As Bob says, "A premium is placed on your customer relations." This even extends to walking the aisles of the supermarket and introducing the idea of supermarket bank to store customers. This obviously requires great flexibility and agility in conducting customer relations.

According to Bob, "I am still learning the job. But, I believe that my background in sociology has been especially helpful for this new type of work. In fact, I'm learning three different organizations at once. One is my branch team of five people. A second is the supermarket where we are located. The third is the main bank. I know there is a formal relationship among the three, but I also know that it is the informal relations, invisible to most, that makes things work. Since this is new, it will take time to sort out all the variables. But I'm confident I will." While still developing his concept of supermarket banking Bob is earning $20,000 - $25,000 in his first year. "It is not a lot, yet, " according to Bob, "but I'm on the ground floor of a major new trend. I'm sure it will pay off in the long run."

What Dave and Bob are demonstrating is that sociology is a highly compatible degree for business. In fact, it is likely to be compatible with most other careers. The question is whether the career you choose involves important relations with others. These profiles have shown that there is more in common than there is different in careers as apparently different as banking and sports equipment sales. The sociological lesson is that it is important to dig beneath the surface to see how things really are, because things -- people -- are not always what they seem. As Dave suggested, "Sociology would be a good leg up on any career."

NOTE:

For more information important to this career see the following chapters in Sociology: A Down to Earth Approach, by James M. Henslin:
      Chapter 4 Social Structure and Social Interaction:
          Macrosociology and Microsociology
      Chapter 7 Bureaucracy and Formal Organizations
      Chapter 14 The Economy: Money and Work
      Chapter 22 Social Change, Technology and the Environment

20.

SOCIOLOGY AND CAREERS
IN THIRD WORLD DEVELOPMENT

Ron Carson is a graduate student. While some would not consider this status a career, many others, particularly those who have been full-time graduate students, would certainly agree that it is. Given that a significant number of people profiled in this book have some kind of post-graduate education, it seems useful to explore the career aspects of graduate study. Ron's case can help you understand your own dreams and options, as well as the obligatory hurdles you must overcome if you are to achieve.

Before proceeding with Ron's profile, I must address the critique, often presented by way of a question, regarding the value of post-graduate education. Some would attempt to criticize the idea of sociology as adequate preparation for a career on the basis that it seems so many with an undergraduate degree in the discipline end up pursuing graduate studies. If the discipline were really career sufficient, so the arguments goes, then no further study would be necessary. In the conclusion to this book several common characteristics are gleaned from these profiles, and they can be summarized in the rejection of the idea that no further study is necessary. To the contrary, those who are really captured by the meanings of sociology understand that life long study, whether formal or informal, is at the heart of the discipline. In addition, consider the following question. To whom do you entrust such important matters as your health, finances, or for that matter your education, to name just a few? We insist on "experts" with a laundry list of credentials. We expect them to be highly prepared and up to date. Consider also our demands on law enforcement, the military, air traffic controllers and fire personnel, in addition to your car mechanic and appliance repair person. The point is, all these positions require education/training of a specialized nature. As consumers, we have come to not only expect it, but we demand it. And so it is that in some applications the undergraduate degree in sociology serves as the foundation for advanced degrees in a variety of fields. Ron Carson is an excellent, and current, example of such.

Ron's story has to go back to the beginning of his undergraduate studies. It is a tale which is somewhat twisted. This is not to say it is bizarre, but his education to date has not occurred in a linear fashion. In the fall of 1986 Ron attended a nearby community college with a rather uninspired commitment to a two-year associate in applied science degree in computer science. According to Ron, "I had done some part-time work in the same steel factory as my father. I decided right away that I did not want

77.

to work in a factory and that I needed to go to school. Basically, I had a tennis friend who played at and attended this junior college, so I decided to do the same. While I chose computer science as a major I was really just getting out of the factory."

There were several effects of this initial experience with college. First, Ron began to develop some broader interests. Second, based on broader interests he became bored with a degree program which he had chosen primarily as a means of staying out of the factory. For these reasons Ron began thinking more along the lines of getting an associates of arts degree and then transferring to a four year program. "At my Dad's suggestion I transferred to another nearby community college where I could follow my emerging interests in mass communication, documentaries and television. However, my horizons had already become expanded and I was really interested in studying in a variety of areas. I would have to say that while my emerging focus was mass communications, I was developing confidence in other areas such as economics, philosophy, history, etc." Thus, in the fall of 1987 Ron was in his second college and, not incidentally, playing tennis on a scholarship which paid his tuition.

It was during 1987-88 that Ron came into contact with a four year school by way of intercollegiate tennis matches. Having met the coach and players, and discussed his interests, Ron decided to transfer in the fall of 1988, after completing his A.A. degree. It was through tennis that Ron was able to make his move after the first year of college, and it was through tennis that he made the contacts which developed into his second move. It was also the case that Ron was interested in the spiritual values of this Christian college. This was significant both personally and in terms of Ron's academic progress. As Ron puts it, "While in the community colleges I became somewhat of an agnostic. After transferring, I found there was much to learn about faith and the concept of a world view." This latter idea noticeably broadened Ron's perspective on himself and the choices he was making. After having lived all his life in the same rural area Ron was becoming aware of the world at large.

During the 1988-89 and 89-90 school years, Ron really branched out and took advantage of many opportunities to expand his horizons. He was still very interested in mass communications, particularly in TV, but was finding that there were a variety of disciplines which had something to offer in this regard. It was in this expanding of his world view that Ron discovered sociology. According to Ron, "I was in a period of time when my interests were going in all directions. My experience at this school was one of being constantly challenged. On the one hand this was very exciting. On the other hand it made it very difficult to choose an academic path. As it turned out, sociology was the discipline that really tied it all together. In fact, I couldn't really escape the reach of sociology. Whether it was television, political science or studying a foreign language, I found in the discipline of sociology a consistent interpretation of people and events."

In the end Ron graduated with a B.A. in sociology and minors in political science and Spanish. This included a six-week program of Spanish language immersion in the Dominican Republic. Little did he know then how important his language proficiency would be in his future. The developing theme of his program was international studies. "I was still interested in television, but there was more purpose in that interest than there used to be. I now had a grasp of some of the issues which a documentary, for example, could reveal. Critical to this realization was an internship I did, through the sociology department, with a major television production company. They literally had projects--some for entertainment or commercial consumption, and some for education--going on all around the world. If you could not understand concepts as simple as culture then you could not function in such work. This made me realize just how much I still had to learn." In some respects this provided additional motivation to not only learn about other cultures, but to acquire a second language.

As he neared graduation, Ron began thinking in earnest about his next step. He had enjoyed the challenges of college, but felt that there was much more to learn. Still present was his interest in television, in particular the documentary. In order to pursue this he needed to get into a mass communications program, though his undergraduate degree was not in that field. As it turned out, a letter from the CEO of the television production company where he had done his internship, as well as an undergraduate transcript which showed breadth and depth, convinced the graduate school of a prestigious Midwest university that Ron was worth the risk. Not only was he admitted to an M.A. program in mass communications in the fall of 1990, but he was given a full tuition waiver plus $500 per month living expenses. In this arrangement, called an assistantship, Ron served the department and individual faculty as a researcher. His sociological skills were most evident in this regard. According to Ron, "I knew how to find things out." In two years Ron was able to complete two semesters of required course-work and a year of work on a major project. Ron's work was good enough to earn summer living support from the university. When combined with his part-time job of tennis instructor at a local club and assistant coach for the university's women's tennis team, Ron was able to live reasonably well and finish his M.A. debt free.

In the spring of 1992 Ron completed his M.A. project, a documentary on the circumstances of Arab-Americans during the Gulf war. According to Ron, "I learned the details of documentary film production in my graduate program. But it was my research skills and world view, as developed in sociology, that provided the insights for my work. In particular, I began to see the media generally as the creator and the responsible entity for many of our viewpoints in society. The news was not merely objective reporting, but a crafted story with a particular slant. Specifically, we tend to see only one side, not the multiple sides of issues or stories. For example, many media presentations on Arab-Americans during that time (the Gulf War) assumed fundamental differences between them (Arab-Americans) and the rest of us. In sociology I had learned how such assumptions, or preconceptions, can be constructed, intentionally or unintentionally, over time. Various media are the primary constructors of such preconceptions. I knew that if I were to dig through the preconceptions then I would get a more accurate understanding of the people involved and the prevailing situation. This was a clear choice that I made, and is a choice which is foundationally sociological. It was also the case that while in school I had encountered students with cultural and ethnic identities quite different from mine, but who were essentially similar to me in many respects. Among these were a Palestinian student and the families I stayed with in the Dominican Republic. I knew them to be different than common stereotypes. It was the means by which they became different to most of us that interested me."

As Ron finished his documentary he began to rethink his role as a media participant, even if it was as critic. "I came to see myself as an observer of the issues; and I felt that I had more to contribute. I wanted to do something, and the Peace Corps seemed to be the opportunity I was looking for." Late that spring Ron began the long process of applying to the Peace Corps. It was concluded in February, 1993 with a two year assignment to Honduras.

The Peace Corps experience was one of "great personal growth," according to Ron. "While I had lot's of feelings and impressions in my two years of service, I learned that I could not always trust them. What I mean is, my preconceptions, based on how I felt about something, were often misleading. Instead, I frequently had to exercise the skill, which really is sociological, of stepping back from the situation in order to see the wide array of variables and processes at work. Stepping back, really is critical." Such variables and processes included details in language, community structure, problem analysis, politics, and informal networks, both at the local level and with in the Peace Corps. "There just wasn't anything about my job that wasn't sociological. My summer study in the Dominican Republic, where I lived with local families, helped me with the acculturation process."

The focus of Ron's Peace Corps work ultimately was to get the local communities to take charge of their own problems, needs, and future. "I had to be very adaptive myself, as I was asking these people to also change. Whatever else sociology is about, it is about change. And here I was trying to make it happen. To do this, I had to learn on the fly. By the time I was done I had learned to direct community development, how to create, lead, and work within teams and then turn over leadership to local citizens, how to monitor and evaluate projects, and how to step outside my areas of expertise into watershed and general environmental protection, and public health. You have to be flexible. You just can't say, that's not my area. You have to have confidence to say, I can figure it out."

By the end of his second year in the Peace Corps Ron was convinced that his future would be in international development and further graduate study. While still in Honduras, Ron studied for the Graduate

Record Exam (GRE) and applied to the University of Pittsburgh's master's program in public and international affairs. In May of 1995 Ron was discharged from the Peace Corps with $5000 and a ticket home. During his tenure in the Peace Corps Ron had received expense money and a $100/month stipend. So, it was necessary that any graduate program be at least partially funded. The University of Pittsburgh responded with a 50% tuition waiver and an assistantship which paid $580 per month for fifteen to twenty hours per week of work.

At the University of Pittsburgh Ron took course-work in a variety of areas, including those which enlarged his research skills such as research design, quantitive and qualitative methods, and evaluation methods. In particular, Ron participated in the research projects of his faculty and department. By networking within the university Ron put himself in a position to access ongoing projects and gain valuable experience in applied research, public policy, development, and funding. "I was learning detailed information and skills such as statistics and econometrics, but I was really learning how to produce opportunities."

Along this latter vein Ron's most important opportunity was produced in the middle summer of his two years at the university. Ron wrote proposals to the University of Pittsburgh's graduate school and Center for Latin American Studies. Together $2800 was granted for living expenses and transportation for research in El Salvador. Specifically Ron was evaluating the effects of United Nations' sponsored education programs on rural adolescents' attitudes and aspirations regarding gender roles, family size, employment, and perceived roles in controlling fertility. This research was conducted employing both survey tools and advanced statistics as well as qualitative methods to develop an affective understanding of adolescent perceptions of the usefulness and effects of the UN programs. "By studying the kids now you begin to get a handle on the future," according to Ron. "It is with the kids that change and development is most likely to occur."

This project cemented Ron's interest in international development. In the summer of 1997 he graduated from the University of Pittsburgh with a Masters of Public and International Affairs degree, and a specialization in economic and social development. And so the question is, now what? Ron did apply and was accepted to Johns Hopkins for doctoral studies in the School of Public Health and Hygiene, Department of Population Dynamics. However, according to Ron, "I have asked them if they would hold my acceptance for a year so that I could test the employment waters. I enjoy school, but I also enjoy the field, and I'm ready for something new. So, I'm planning on going to Washington, DC, that's where the action is in international development, and we'll see what happens."

The attitude expressed in this last statement can be disconcerting for some. Obviously Ron does not have a "job," but he is confident about his future. He is prepared. Much of this perspective, according to Ron, is attributable to "...my studies which always challenged me to adapt to the situation at hand. This is one of the real strengths of sociology. Of course, languages are necessary, as are research skills, but I would never have seen language and research as necessary had I not first been through sociology." Finally, according to Ron, "NETWORK! Get to know as many people as you can. It is through them that opportunities are won or lost. I learned that in Intro!"

Postscript: Within about three months of graduating Ron was hired as an Administrative Assistant with the World Bank in Washington, D.C. He works within the department of External Affairs for the Latin American and Caribbean Region. So far, his work consists of drafting letters (in Spanish), conducting assigned research, and reviewing and distributing relevant news and media commentaries to bank staff. Entry level pay for such work is in the neighborhood of $10/ hour. However, according to Ron, "It's not about money. It's about being in a place where one might be able to make a difference. And, the networking here is unbelievable. I have encountered alumni and friends from each school I have attended. This is simply how you move around within the bank."

Additionally, Ron is a finalist for a two year overseas assignment with the Population-Environment Fellows program. If accepted he will be back in the field in Equador, Peru, or Nicaragua. According to Ron, "I would be working with Nature Conservancy and serve other NGO's (Non-Governmental Organizations) in order to enhance protection of a National Park. The key is to make such protection beneficial and more attractive to communities in the park's buffer zone. Tools in accomplishing this would include community development in coordination with others in water, sanitation, public health, agriculture and family planning outreach. Watershed protection and other uses of the forest's resources would be placed under local community control in the hope that this will eventually lead to sustained protection." While still pending, this program pays $24,000 per year plus health insurance and other benefits.

NOTE:

For more information to this career, see the following chapters in *Sociology: A Down to Earth Approach,* by James M. Henslin:

21.

SOCIOLOGY AND CAREERS
IN THE COMPUTER INDUSTRY

Chris Sanders is a technical writer for a leading software company specializing in network operating systems and internet applications. Whenever you have clicked on the "Help" button in an effort to figure out how to do something on your computer then you have entered into the territory of end-user documentation. Chris is one of those who writes the directions. Before giving Chris the "Bronx Cheer" for some of the really lame "Help" directions you have read, you should know that Chris's focus is on directions for the installation of network operating systems. He is writing to and for people in the computer services department of your college or university.

At 27 years of age Chris is part of a new generation of software technical writers. According to Chris, "The work used to be basically journalistic. The technical writer would talk with the engineers and then generate a set of directions. The problem with many of the directions was that they were written from the point of view of the software engineer and not the end-user or customer. In addition the technical writer did not necessarily understand all the "in's and out's" of using the software. Now the technical writer not only interviews the software engineer, he must be able to run the product, know how it works, be able to use it and, perhaps most importantly, understand what the product is supposed to do. In this way I have become an end-user myself, and I can write directions from the customers point of view."

Chris's journey to his position as a first year technical writer in a cutting-edge high tech industry is one which, according to Chris, "... would be very difficult to map out in detail ahead of time. While I've always had an interest in computers, at least since I was in junior high, I do not have a degree in computer science. Instead, I have a B.A. in English and Sociology and an M.A. in Interdisciplinary Studies. However, I believe that the path I've taken has uniquely prepared me for a career on the cutting edge of technology. Further, it is amazing how often I find myself employing the lessons of sociology or English as I encounter situations or problems in this industry."

That "edge," to which Chris refers, is by definition a point of change, a time when something new is occurring. " To be able to see and anticipate the dynamics of change, to have a useful perspective on the relationships of many people, and to have insight into the patterns of organizational behavior are all extremely important to making it in the environment of high technology. In addition, you must also be able to anticipate how that cutting and technological edge will impact end-users; that is, a person who merely encounters the technology at home on their PC, or in the grocery store, gas station, or ATM." In this respect, the cutting edge in technology creates a whole array of edges in society at large. Sometimes those edges are doorways to exciting new possibilities. But those same edges may create a sense of fear, dread, or stress. The differences can be illustrated in the way children seem to rush headlong into something like the Internet, while mom and dad can't even figure out how to turn the machine on. It is not that they actually cannot understand, it is the anomic stress of such experiences which can keep some people from even trying.

So how is it that Chris came to be in this kind of work, and to have done so without a degree in computer science? As already mentioned Chris has always wanted to be involved with computers; at least since junior high days when the wonders of computers were first reaching into public schools. However, according to Chris, "Most computer science programs in college had a significant emphasis on math, and I just wasn't that interested in math." Instead Chris found he had and interest and a facility for English, both literature and writing, and as Chris says, "I was good at it (English)."

The transition to sociology was a product of both insights in English, and his continuing desire for a more formal or scientific mode of analysis. "In English literature and in writing the most frequent topic by far is human relationships. In time I began to see patterns to these relationships. Sometimes a piece of literature presents relationships which are so implausible as to be unbelievable. If a story is to get anywhere there must be an understanding of how people really behave. Sociology provides this understanding, and did so in a manner that fit with my overarching scientific bent. It provided ideas and methods which enhanced my understanding of the patterns I had been noticing. At the time my contact with sociology had been merely through general education courses such as SOC 101. I had no initial intention of adding sociology as a major. But I saw that there was developing a useful fit between English and sociology, and I was in a position where I could certainly use the hours.. So, as you can see, I wasn't just overwhelmed, at least at first, by the potential or career implications of sociology. It fit with what I was doing and what I needed. However, I must say, that it (sociology) has turned out to be much more helpful in day-to-day life, including my career, than I ever thought it might." Such benefits became evident as Chris took his first career steps while simultaneously entering graduate school.

Chris spent nearly the next three years in the far west studying for his masters degree. " I was in an interdisciplinary M.A. program in which I combined English literature, composition and sociology. My thesis was on John Keats and I had to combine all three areas of study. I ended up showing how Keats' writings and final products were influenced by groups and movements in society at large. The point was that Keats was not writing in a vacuum, nor was he independent of the society in which he lived. We sometimes think of writers as being independent, but that misunderstands both who they are and what they do."

While working on his degree Chris served as a teaching assistant, teaching classes primarily in English composition and business writing. For this he received a full tuition waiver for his graduate studies and a stipend of about $10,000 per year. While the courses Chris taught were "canned"-- that is, there was a pre-determined syllabus, course objectives etc.-- Chris said, " I took any opportunity to let the students know of the sociological realities they were encountering. In fact, they needed to know they could not escape the sociological realities they were encountering."

In his last year of graduate studies, and while writing his thesis, Chris took a job with Kinko's. According to Chris, " I took the job basically for the additional income," about $17,000. This job, however, became what amounted to a first career step which not only put him in touch with networked computer systems, but also put to the test the sociological ideas and principles which he had both studied and taught. Kinko's was developing its own services in the area of desktop publishing, resume writing, and other professional services especially adapted to network computer systems. Chris was hired as a Manager of Computer Services and Desktop Publishing. The installation and running of a store network was his primary responsibility. According to Chris, " While an increasing number of people now use or own computers, there is still a significant amount of uneasiness about using computers. This situation calls for careful management of customer relations, especially in the area of rental computers. One has to understand that what may be second nature to themselves is quite foreign, and even threatening to others." Chris also began to perceive the organization of work in new ways. He began to see that fitting people together to form a business required another form of careful management. However, this is not management in the typical business sense. It is management of the social situation. "I began to see the different roles of customer, service and technical personnel, management, etc."

Chris worked with Kinko's for about a year until he completed his M.A. At that time his alma mater called with needs he could fulfill. The college where he earned his B.A. needed expertise in network installation and management. The college was having its first experience with the internet and E-mail. There was also an opportunity to teach in the English department. According to Chris, this job was a natural next step from Kinko's. He liked the college environment and had significant responsibility for the college's move into and development of its internet capacities. The combined position offered a salary of $25,000, and a wealth of practical organizational experiences. Such opportunities included far more than simply installing and running machines. "I was constantly meeting with people who wanted access to the technology, but who in some cases had no idea of its uses or potential. There were also those who believed they had all the answers, and were not particularly interested in my questions. My role in the organization, apart from my personal identity and separate from other roles, is what stands out from that experience. While I experienced the organization daily, and interpersonally, I was also able to step back from the action and see how my role, and my performance of that role, fit in." In such situations one is perhaps in a better position to understand the behavior of others, as actors within the organization, rather than separate individuals. Management, in this sense, does not mean the exercise of authority within the organization, but rather careful attention to the relationships. In small settings, such as the college, it is often the case that role and interpersonal relations become mixed or confused. Chris's ability to step back was critical in his eventual success in establishing the college as a local internet provider to the wider community, as well as through developing the college's network for intra and internet services.

While he would have preferred to stay in the college context, Chris moved on after about sixteen months. Much had been accomplished in that time, in particular Chris's abilities to work in and through an organization. However, due to significant organizational stresses Chris began looking for other opportunities. It is here that Chris accomplished a career development task in a most unique way. He did his entire job search via the internet. According to Chris, if he could not stay where he was, he wanted to make sure his next step was progress. He decided that his immediate future should be with the cutting-edge companies, such as Hewlett-Packard, Intel, Novel, Microsoft, etc. At that time most computer companies, though not most companies generally, were fully internet accessible. His job search thus meant that he accessed companies in which he was interested and submitted resumés, via the internet. His formal position of network administrator and instructor in English was eventually matched with the job he now had as a technical writer. However, what companies were really looking for were people who could translate the technical side of computer work--in this case the installation, running and writing of network programming--into end-user needs, such as network functions, client services and administration.

Chris believes that his education and work experiences came together in a way to uniquely qualify him for the position of technical writer. Most would not consider English and computer science as especially compatible. But in this case they are. However, being qualified does not equal job performance. It is here that Chris credits his sociological insights, at least in part, with his ability to find his way around this new organization. It is the manner and success you have in managing the various relationships of work that constitutes the organization. The organization, as an organization, does not exist without such relationships. Otherwise it's just an idea of an organization or a chart on the wall.

In talking about his work Chris uses the following kind of descriptors: "intense, meetings, competitive, meetings, vision, meetings, Internet time, meetings, upheaval, meetings, and change." The point is, while the work must include the technical ability to actually install, by hand, a network, the ability to do so does not determine one's life in the organization. According to Chris, " The majority of the day is spent in meetings. Since any project has multiple components in order for the final product to be accomplished, departments must be in sync. Problems arise when synchronization does not occur. To some degree this is a function of different departments being geographically separate, as in different states or even countries. Even with the telephone, FAX, e-mail, and video-conferencing it is amazing how much interdepartmental strife there is because we cannot actually see face-to-face. The interpersonal relationship is just that important."

All the above dynamics are further animated by a new computer business concept: "Internet time." Internet time is actually a function of world wide economic competition. Internet time is an acceleration of business practices. In this case, according to Chris, "...what used to take from three to four years from concept to product must now be accomplished in three to twelve months." Such intensity in time means that work relations must be smooth, functional and in "sync." According the Chris,"...this means that while you are engaged in the technical details of your department's work, you must also be aware of how other departments are working and how you will work together." For those who are unwilling to do so, or simply just misunderstand the significance of doing so, then work will not progress. As Chris says, " If I have any advantage at all it is that I am constantly noticing how the organization works; what works and what doesn't. I can be detached, yet also part of the work." This ultimately provides a hint of efficiency of action, or work. By carefully observing, or "noticing", as Chris puts it, inefficient or ineffective relations can be avoided and productive ones pursued. " The point," according to Chris, " is not that I am working as a sociologist within this company, because I am not. However, as mentioned earlier, I have come to appreciate the insights I have, in ways that I simply could not have imagined while in school."

After only 10 months as a technical writer Chris makes a base pay of about $50,000. Added to this are a benefits package of about $5,000 and bonuses of from $2,000 to $3,000. While the income is certainly more than he made previously, it is not necessarily the most important factor. Chris has already survived a company downsizing move of over 1000 personnel. " You are reminded just how volatile the industry is," according to Chris. "You must anticipate and adapt to change. Those who do not may be in for a rude awakening." So, Chris suggests that the college life may yet be in his future. But now he is happy and challenged by this kind of work.

As for specific advice to current undergraduates Chris worries that in retrospect the "cliché's" do seem appropriate. He wishes that there was some more specific formula, but in his case he does not see one. Instead he says, " stay in school." The important point here is to finish what you begin because you cannot be sure, in an ever-changing environment, just how things will work out. Instead, you must simply be ready, and school promotes this. Second, Chris believes that pursuing the M.A. was a good move. The additional education, even in a field not specifically or directly related, is a positive signal, particularly in the developing high tech companies. Such companies are growing and changing so quickly that bright, adaptable people, from a variety of academic backgrounds are desired. It must be remembered that only a few short years ago technical writers did not really know how to use the product. Further, there seemed to be little or no organizational motivation for such skill. Finally, and perhaps most importantly, do not be fixed on a specific career plan. Chris was somewhat reluctant to give advice because, " I could not have mapped out what happened to me in my career thus far. So, it might not be useful for others." However Chris's career is more typical of the cutting-edge; that place where change is expected. " The important thing is to be ready."

NOTE:

For additional information important to this career, see the following chapters in *Sociology: A Down to Earth Approach,* by James M. Henslin:

Chapter 7 Bureaucracy and Formal Organization
Chapter 14 The Economy: Money and Work
Chapter 17 Education: Transferring Knowledge and Skills
Chapter 22 Social Change, Technology, and the Environment

22.

SOCIOLOGY AND CAREERS
IN MILITARY INTELLIGENCE

In 1986 Chad Christopher had a National Guard tuition scholarship for any state college or university and "an urge to get away from home." Education was not really the objective. According to Chad, "I had no clear sense of where I was heading when it came time for college. I was not focused on the future at all. In fact, because I was in boot camp I missed out on my freshman orientation; not a real good start." Three years later Chad "found himself" to be majoring in geography. "Actually I had kind of a knack for it (geography) and I was developing an interest in other cultures. I was also beginning to think, however remotely, of becoming an officer, and geography seemed to be a compatible degree. Today Chad is an officer, a Marine Corps Captain to be exact, serving at the Pentagon in the National Military Joint Intelligence Center. To accomplish this required a change of school and discipline to develop the focus necessary to move forward in life.

While Chad had spent three years at a state school and had begun to study geography, he was still only a sophomore. At this time, Chad became aware of a new football program which was starting up at a smaller, private liberal arts college near his home town. Having played football in high school and remaining interested in the game, and still being somewhat adrift where he was, Chad decided to transfer. "Really, I transferred in order to get in a couple of years of football. But the result was that I became much more focused. It was as if I began to awaken from a slumber. The catalyst was sociology. The courses I took had a most profound influence on me. They *forced* me to *think* about what I believed."

The result of this awakening was Chad's decision to major in sociology. "In sociology classes I simply could not get by with glancing over the topics. I found myself diving in and exploring the issues, more than I ever had before. In Intro, I had to keep a journal. Every week we had to write one typed page on any topic of our choosing. Now, that may seem like a simple task, but you can't do it if you're not thinking, at least a little bit. And, as the course went on, I noticed that I began to think of things, all kinds of things, in ways related to what we are studying; sociology. It really is amazing when you notice that you're thinking sociologically."

In two years, Chad played football and got his life into focus. He decided that he wanted to go into the Air Force, but was not admitted. He had been an athlete, and football had taken its toll. However, through a friend he learned about opportunities in the Marines, though he was not certain if he wanted to go that route. In December of 1991, Chad graduated and took a job stacking a semi at a local warehouse. According to Chad, "This was definitely not what I wanted to do after all the education I had received. So I decided to continue in school and in March of 1992 I began a master's program in sports management at the United States Sports Academy in Alabama. I just completed that degree this past summer (1997). Sport is something I have always loved and the degree program was a way of staying at it. I also found that all the attention in sports on teams, coaching, and organization were actually quite compatible with my degree in sociology."

At the same time Chad began the master's program he decided to re-examine options with the Marines. The result was an application to Officer Candidate School (OCS). "The Marines are interested in people with education because they need people who can and are willing to learn. They also want people who have demonstrated leadership by being involved. In my last two years of college I not only played football but I served in the National Guard, was President of the local chapter of the Fellowship of Christian Athletes, and developed a decent GPA. I also fulfilled an internship at the Senior Bowl football game as part of my masters program."

In January of 1993 Chad began OCS. According to Chad, "For me this was a real gut-check, mentally, physically, and spiritually. For the first time, I was surrounded by people who had their program together. They could think, write, and communicate. Learning for them was a passion." While this new environment had the capacity to be intimidating, and sometimes was, Chad now understands that he really was prepared for it. "My experiences as an undergrad, in particular my studies in sociology, were great preparation for OCS. I had learned about leadership in class and in practice, and this was the objective of OCS."

The OCS environment is intense. As Chad puts it, " It was often anomic." The intensity, however, is in the relationships, and this is also where the sociological imagination makes a difference. The discipline surrounds one with tools which allow, or even cause, one to step outside the situation at hand. By doing so you are now in a position to see the phenomenon at hand (the words of your peers, for example) from different perspectives. According to Chad, "I feel that my background in sociology caused me to be extra aware. I was always noticing, whether it was the organization, how people lived, or what was going on beneath the surface. This was ultimately critical to my ability to persevere. You see, the Corps is made up of people from so many different backgrounds that it is very easy to be prejudiced to each other. But for the Corps to work, it is critical that we build deep, trusting relationships. A bond must be created. Those who cannot bridge their differences will not succeed (35% of the OCS class did not make it). Almost anyone can learn the detail of the military, but it is the relationship that makes it viable."

One of the interests which Chad developed focused on international relations and culture. The same ability to build relationships among a diverse collection of people within the Corps is also absolutely necessary in international settings. "This was one of the reasons the Vietnam War was so frustrating for Americans. We simply did not and seemingly could not develop a meaningful understanding of the Vietnamese. It was in fact, according to Chad, "A course in the sociology of war which began to synthesize my interests. I saw the military and war through much different eyes. The book we read, *A Bright Shining Lie*, documented the significance of culture for the effective functioning of the military. It is interesting to note that one of my first classes at OCS had *A Bright Shining Lie* as required reading. I felt as if I were somewhat ahead of the game, having already read and studied that book. My degree in sociology was already paying dividends. And, I was beginning to develop an interest that would lead me to military intelligence."

In ten weeks, Chad graduated from OCS and was commissioned as a second lieutenant. Next it was six months of Basic School, "where I really learned to be an officer and a rifle platoon commander. The objective is to be able to lead forty men into combat. "The issues here are absolutely sociological. Soldiers must be able to perform under duress and be in coordination with each other. The relationships among members of the platoon must on the one hand respect the specific roles each member must fulfill, while on the other hand develop beyond the roles in order to create interpersonal loyalty." According to Chad, "You must always be observant of those under your command. In this way you can select appropriate strategies for your objectives. You see, there is always   more than one way of getting things done. Sometimes you use the formal structures of the Corps, while at other times you must use informal interpersonal means."

After Basic School Chad had an opportunity to more vigorously pursue his developing interest in cross cultural and international issues. The means of opportunity was military intelligence. The tasks were quite varied, but centered around providing immediate and accurate information to and for a base colonel regarding general security clearances. According the Chad, "You really had very little time to make the right decision. In this position you have to grasp situations quickly and decide accurately." Eventually Chad completed the Basic Officer Intelligence Course. In this he began to learn the larger picture of the United States intelligence community as a whole. This included agencies such as the FBI, CIA, the National Security Agency, and the role and function of satellites.

By October 1995 Chad was back in training at Camp Lejeune, NC. "While I had focused on intelligence it is important to understand that everyone in the Marines is a soldier, and we all have multiple roles." The training included assignment to a artillery unit, desert training, and cold weather training as infantry. Of particular interest was Chad's opportunity to go to Norway and engage in NATO exercises with German, Italian and British military personnel. "I learned just how differently a relatively common situation could be interpreted depending on one's point of view. This obviously made sociological sense, but it is not interesting when you initially encounter it. This obviously made sociological sense, but it is most interesting when you actually encounter it. Among the specific perspectives, I got a reality check on the Soviet threat. My European peers were much more aware and sensitive to it than I was. Through this I learned how important it is to simply listen to others rather than follow stereotypes. From a security or intelligence point of view you must have an understanding of a variety of other perspectives. You realize your perspective is only one among several."

Chad later helped train units which were heading to the Mediterranean. According to Chad, " We would practice a variety of intelligence scenarios. We wanted to know, ahead of time, what to do in different situations. We also involved different organizations, such as the CIA, the State Department, and the International Red Cross. Not only do cultures vary by nation, but they also vary by organization. You must be sensitive to and expect differences. The ones who also simply assume that others will perceive as they do, are the ones who will who fail the task of intelligence."

By October of 1996 Chad was at a point of decision. He would either move on within the Marines, or return to civilian life. His decision was to stay on, due in large part to an opportunity for advancement. According to Chad, "I applied for and was accepted as a Marine Liaison Officer for the National Military Joint Intelligence Center at the Pentagon. My role is to support the Intelligence Estimates Branch. Essentially, this is an Alert Center, in which intelligence is provided for the Joint Chiefs of Staff, the President, CIA, National Security Agency, and others in the broad field of intelligence and security. We work with regional analysts from all parts of the world and have specialists in terrorism and spies. Based on these resources we try to anticipate and be prepared to respond to crises anywhere in the world. For example, the evacuation of Sierra Leone, Zaire (now the Congo), Cambodia, and information on groups such as rebels in Peru. You may not and often don't know the specific answer or piece of information requested. But you must know how to find it. Further, you must see the information in context. Out of context your information may simply be worthless."

In October of 1997 Chad took on his latest assignment. He became part of a National Intelligence Support Team (he is still a Marine liaison Officer). As part of a team of four
such a team is sent to a particular Crisis Center. In Chad's case Bosnia. According to Chris, "On the ground the liaison reports up to the Pentagon and back down to people on the line." In a very real sense Chad is in the role of a participant observer. He is gathering primary data by participating at the local level. For example, "I have learned just how lasting the scars of the Bosnian crisis will be. It is my job to clearly and accurately reflect the local point of view. I really am a sociologist on the ground."

During this last assignment Chad was promoted to Captain. With a total of twelve years experience and his new rank, he is paid at $55,000 per year plus significant benefits. As a lieutenant he was earning about $45,000. According to Chad, "I believe that my degree in sociology and my career have been and will continue to be highly compatible. In sociology I learned how to notice and assess a situation, which is precisely what I must do now. Most important, whatever else life in the military is, it is a life of figuring out how to get along with others in order to get the job done. Sociology couldn't be any more appropriate."

NOTE:
For more information important to this career. See the following chapters in
Sociology: A Down to Earth Approach, by James M. Henslin:

23.

SOCIOLOGY AND CAREERS IN ENTREPRENEURSHIP

Eileen Caldwell and Nadia Miller illustrate the potential sociology holds for the entrepreneur. In addition, they demonstrate the potential of sociology for women in business. While there is no substitute for quality in work and product, and both Eileen and Nadia are absolutely committed to this; entrepreneurial sociology is an open door to women in business. The two cases to follow track their entrepreneurial experiences as well as demonstrate the breadth and depth of careers in sociology.

Eileen Caldwell is both a Ph.D. in sociology and a classic entrepreneur who began writing proposals in a loft in her home, moved to the basement for space, then set up offices in the suburbs, and eventually went uptown in a major metropolitan area. She runs and is the sole stock holder in a research and consulting business which at any one time will have from fifteen to nineteen "equal partner" employees and annual revenues of $1.5 million (1997). Her business typically has forty active contracts, some in the $200,000 per year range, and churns out contract proposals at about one per month. "We have a high rate of success, " according to Eileen, "about 75% of proposals are awarded." So, how does this happen for someone who began college majoring in religion? Actually, there is no single answer. Rather this is a story of many subplots including family, education, and opportunity.

Eileen began college in 1967 in a special liberal arts honors program of a Midwestern state university. Her initial foci were religion and physics. " I was interested in the issues presented in religion, and I was good at quantative disciplines. However, I decided to follow my interests, so I dropped physics and focused more on religion. The events of 1968 changed all this. King and Kennedy were assassinated and it was in sociology that these and other related events were being discussed. So, I changed my major to sociology and math." By December of 1970 Eileen graduated. She had been married earlier that year, in April. This is important because Eileen's commitment to family and relationships has significantly shaped her choices and results.

Immediately after graduation Eileen embarked on what she called, "an awful experience" in public education. "I went to Kalamazoo and taught junior high math in an inner city school to which a number of white students were being bussed. It was scary and difficult to deal with the pervasive conflict. But I did stick out the semester (January - May 1971) and even came back and taught summer school." Among other things,

Eileen learned to adapt and to problem solve. " I was certainly using skills I had learned from sociology, even though I was teaching math." For example, Eileen ran a school store which sold miscellaneous items to students, and used that experience to teach basic math concepts.

By the summer of 1971 Eileen's husband was wanting to complete his doctorate and suggested that she go back to school as well. She agreed and in the fall of 1971 she enrolled in a master's program which eventually led to the doctorate. "The program I was in was actually a fast track program and I was finished with the Ph.D. by 1974. In one sense the Ph.D. was a competitive thing with my husband and others. And I had received a lot of encouragement since my undergraduate days, including from my parents, to pursue whatever I wanted. So, I pursued the M.A. and Ph.D. and specialized in research methods, statistics, and social psychology. Neverless, I can't say that sociology was actually a calling for me. Rather, as a discipline, it was well centered for the time. It made sense among the events which were transpiring. However, while I had the Ph.D., I also had daughter, and no job."

Eileen initially thought she would like to go into academics. The problem was that she and her husband could not get jobs in the same place. In time Eileen's husband took a federal job with the Bureau of Land Management. Eileen began looking outside academics and took a Manpower job which paid $12,000 a year. "Basically I just collected data on people who came in for our services. Later I made forms for data collection. It was pretty simple stuff, but this was fine with me as I was ready for a break from scholarship. I just worked and raised my daughter." This job lasted about eight months.

At about this time the federal government began pouring significant sums of money into various forms of local law enforcement through the Law Enforcement Assistance Administration (LEAA). Eileen took a job as the head of research for an inner city organization which sponsored community based programming in line with LEAA. "In order for us to know if the programming was effective we had to evaluate. To do this well required both a pre-test and post-test of the programming. Unfortunately, applying a research design in practice is not the same as designing one in graduate school." In this case, the project became delayed for six months because the community pre-test could not get done. Eventually the project proceeded, but was shut down before the post-test could conducted. According to Eileen, " This project produced several kinds of results. One, I realized that any project has multiple interests. If you don't pay attention to these it is entirely possible to fail, even if you are doing good work. Two, it produced a lot of strong emotions. I felt guilty. The project had failed. So, there I was, 24 years old, out of work again, and with a strong sense of guilt.

Eileen's response to this situation was to "become an entrepreneur." By this time Eileen had two children and a strong interest in raising them. "I preferred a job which would allow me to make my own time for work and family, and I decided that I needed to be more aggressive in creating my own work opportunities." For clarification a contract is offered by some agency on a competitive proposal basis. Eileen was becoming entrepreneurial in that she was now working as an independent contractor, just as anyone would do in the business world. The first result was a contract job with the local regional council of governments. The contract called for research on the administration of juvenile justice in the metropolitan area. Of particular interest was the variability of practices among judges and prosecuting attorneys. This provided approximately seventy-five percent full-time work for one year. Additionally, she won another small grant for an evaluation project. One important point of this was that Eileen was beginning to generate a cash-flow. Another was that Eileen began to reconsider the kind of work she was doing and her role in it. " I decided it was time to incorporate, to really go into business". The product was a research and training business with Eileen, her husband, and her father (who had entreprenual experience) serving on the board of directors. This was 1975. Over the next five years Eileen "...did lots of little projects; enough to keep the money flowing. Most importantly, I learned how to operate a business, which really meant dealing effectively with people. I was able to both support myself and help out within the community. I really liked this, and felt good about working with people." This was a significant change from the results of the LEAA project.

While progress was being made in her research and training business Eileen decided in 1980 to move with the times (at least for a while) and got into the growing computer field. " I put the research and training business on hold and gave selling computers a try. I really wasn't good at it, selling only one in three months. I was kind of disillusioned with this particular kind of encounter with the business community. There seemed to be no real social conscience in business, and I felt some discrimination against my Ph.D. The effect of this was to confirm that I really liked sociology and research." So, Eileen decided to get out of computer sales, but not until she had secured a contract for the research and training business.

The contract this time was with the Federal Emergency Management Agency (FEMA). The contract generally called for Eileen to do emergency preparedness training, including nuclear war survival, flood plain management, etc. The geographic area covered eleven states and required a lot of travel. " Basically," according to Eileen, " I worked much like a professor with a curriculum which had already been prepared by the Feds. However, every locale was different and I had to learn how to work among a diverse populations."

While on the one hand the business was developing in a positive way, there were impending challenges-- Eileen's marriage ended in divorce and the business was reincorporated. " I had five staff people and we all worked for FEMA. But it all went away in two weeks as the Feds pulled our contract in a budget cutting move. This was the beginning of a very introspective time. I was 35 years old, unemployed, again (for about one year), and not really sure just what to do. My response was to become much more proactive about my own career. Until the I had really been reactive to people and events around me."

One of Eileen's decisions was to no longer be a one-contract business. She needed a "larger" base, and this required multiple contracts. "Until then I had not really invested in my business. This time I sunk dollars into it and bought a computer, printer and other office stuff. It was 1986 and I began writing proposals, frantically. My primary competition was university research centers and it was not easy to break in. You do have to know people and what they really want in an RFP (request for proposal). It really was an emotional experience waiting on contracts." One strength of Eileen's business was that she had almost no overhead, and therefore her proposals were very competitive. "The result was one contract with Job Training which I've had renewed each year since 1986. Now we typically service about forty contracts per year, and turn out about one new proposal per month."

After over eleven years Eileen is well-established as a practitioner and researcher in sociology. Plus, she has demonstrated a great capacity to learn and adapt on the fly. This has allowed Eileen to progress from times when she struggled with guilt over failure to now exercising significant confidence. As Eileen says, "You must have confidence. This allows you to take on any project within reason When asked, you must be able to answer the question, 'What are you good at?' In my case I know that I am a good researcher. I have the tools." But in addition you must have a strong and productive work ethic. In a client-driven environment, you must demonstrate your skills and be productive, for there may be no other opportunities. According to Eileen, "Students often feel that in order to get the job done they must talk about the issue, problem or project. Actually, listening is most important for clients. Your responsibility is to be a confident reactor to various situations, including your clients. A positive result is that you will really know your client, your client will become your friend and you will be able to fulfill their needs. You really are in the position of giving to others." A tangible product is a financially successful business. According to Eileen, "You can't be afraid to make money. In fact, your ability to do that is what others depend on." Eileen now makes approximately $150,000 per year in salary and benefits.

It has been a long and varied career for Eileen. She had experienced guilt over failure and joy in success. The secret, according to Eileen, can be found in the pivotal social relationships we all have. "You must be in supportive family relationships. Your career is not simply your own--you must be in league with others, including family, colleagues, and clients. It is these relationships that your values are played out, and through which your career develops."

Nadia Miller says, " I do enjoy what I do. I'm never bored in the business because there are always new projects. My work is both exciting and fun." Nadia's work has included creating, owning, and running both not-for-profit and for-profit business as well as teaching a full load in sociology at the university level. With a dual career path spanning 20 years, Nadia now has a combined income of approximately $120,000 per year. "While I certainly do work hard, I feel that sociology has been a field which is trending toward women. By this I mean, in sociology there is an openness to women which in turn produces opportunity for women. The result is that you are ultimately evaluated on what you can do, not on who you are." More to the point, what has Nadia done?

From 1968-1971 Nadia "marched" through a B.A. program in Sociology. "I was originally interested in social work, but soon realized that I didn't really want to do that. However, sociology was coming into vogue; it was booming. On one hand it was close to social work, but it was more analytical. And it was interesting." Upon completion of the B.A. Nadia received significant encouragement from faculty and she eventually decided to pursue graduate study. By 1973 she had earned her master's degree in sociology and was on track to engage what she calls, "the profession of sociology."

Initially Nadia engaged the profession in applied settings such as research supervisor and data analyst for evaluations of the Governor's Justice Commission's Safe Streets Impact Program. Other positions and projects included research supervisor for a study on perceptions of time at the University of Sind, Pakistan, consultant and evaluator of an employee assistance program with General Electric, and political polling.

In 1975 Nadia and her husband created a not-for-profit institute for research. Today it has an annual budget of approximately $500,000. The institute generates grant dollars from the state department of labor and industry, and then develops programming for the training of displaced workers and workers in transition. Other programming includes vocational computer training and teaching people who are eligible for government funding. At present, Nadia has little direct involvement with the institute, but still serves as its treasurer. According to Nadia," In the early days of the institute there were a number of things to learn and they all had to be learned while on the job. These included grant writing, networking, and doing research in a competitive atmosphere. Simply having a good idea is insufficient. You must find ways to put them into action."

While the institute of research continues to this day, there were, according to Nadia, limitations due to its status as a non-profit organization. So, in 1980 Nadia and her husband created a for-profit research entity. "This freed us to pursue research opportunities wherever they might lead." In new form grants and contracts were pursued in both the public (i.e. state and local government) and private (business and industry) sectors. Over the years this for-profit entity has grown to the point where it employees 30-35 researchers, teachers, librarians, and others, produces annual revenues of approximately $5 million and has headquarters in a renovated school building with about 75,000 square feet of space.

Of particular note is that this research entity has special status within the state as a socio-economic restricted business (SERB). According to Nadia, " Essentially SERB's are minority-owned businesses. Since the beginning I have been both owner and president." The minority status is that of gender, female. "We were not a SERB business from the start, that came later. My focus has never been our status as a minority business. Rather, the focus has always been, and must continue to be good work, and a reputation for good work. That reputation is critical since it is the foundation for the next contract." At times Nadia seems unsure of the exact impact or benefit of SERB status. But the fact is, according to Nadia, "Given the current contracting climate companies need minority participation. Being A SERB does help, however, when putting together an RFP (Request for Proposal)."

The success of the business rests upon a consistent ability to productively compete for grants. As Nadia says, " Our business is grant driven." In this case most grants are awarded through the state; nearly 100%. This requires attention to three important details. Networking establishes pivotal relationships. It does matter by whom and by what means you are known. Networking is much more than simply meeting people. Networking is intentionally creating relationships with people in specific roles of specific structures. A second detail is preparation. You must thoroughly know with whom you are working and the important details of the work to be done. Networking contributes to preparation, but hard work is always necessary. Because of the variety of projects resourcing, the third detail is a necessary skill. You may not initially know the specifics of some potential project; but by resourcing you seek out those who do know. This takes the form of hiring certain employees, subcontracting, or research. You may not know the answer, but you need to know how to find it.

The variety of projects Nadia's business has addressed is quite impressive. The following list is only a sampling:

Study of Community Development Block Grant Agencies
Data Collection and Analysis of Rural Public Transportation
Needs Assessment and Evaluation for Alcohol Treatment
Nutrition Education Needs Assessment
Department of Public Welfare Food Stamps Survey
Market Research (various companies)
Attitude Surveys (various companies)
Evaluation Research, Child Daycare Services
Strategic Planning, County Economic Opportunities Council
Assessment of Aftercare Services for Delinquent Youth

One of the more recent and on-going projects had been the establishment of a substance abuse and health information center for the state department of health. This clearinghouse provides library and information services for an array of state agencies charged with addressing substance abuse and health issues. This has been on-going since 1991.

Earlier it was noted that Nadia was a dual career professional. Since 1978 Nadia has taught sociology at the college and university levels. She has risen from instructor to full Professor and has also served as an associate provost. The balancing of education and business roles is no simple task. However, Nadia seems to have managed, and even thrives with such responsibilities. As a past president of the Society for Applied Sociology Nadia wrote a regular "Presidents Column" for the society's newsletter. In her last column Nadia addressed this dual career question head on:

Given the scope of both of these endeavors, some of you may wonder how I maintain both of these career paths-I sometimes wonder myself. I was recently asked... " What connections do you see between your academic profession and your business endeavors?" This query was part of an interview being conducted for an article in the magazine *Together*, a publication of the Foundation for Independent Colleges, Inc. The feature of the summer issue of this magazine was on faculty who are also involved in a business.

For me, the answer to this question came quickly-I foremost see myself as a *sociologist.* Thus, I am not simply a university professor who teaches classes and advises students, nor am I simply an owner and operator of a service business. I see all the various endeavors and projects in which I become engaged as opportunities to apply the sociological knowledge and skills that I have learned in training and experience. Therefore, even though it might look like I have compartmentalized my life into a dual career track, in reality, I am engaged in the profession of sociology. Indeed, there are many ways in which the experiences I have in academia enhance my business and vice-versa. In the classroom I am able to provide very concrete examples from the "real world" along with offering internship possibilities for students.

However, there are some aspects to being in business for which sociology did not prepare me. Such things as figuring payroll, purchasing insurance coverage, preparing for audits, paying taxes, writing contracts, contending with lawsuits, dealing with bankers, working with building contractors, maintenance and cleaning staff, etc. All of these are part of the business enterprise today, once you get beyond the "mom and pop" shop. In the case of our business, these are aspects that have been "learned on the job" and have required the establishment of a network other professionals who provide their expertise/service to us on a routine basis.

In conclusion, what does this all mean? Essentially, I want to emphasize that we should all think of ourselves as sociologists and with that as our primary identity, we can then talk about the ways in which we apply the knowledge and skills of our profession. Too often, as sociologists, we are hesitant to identify ourselves as such. We either become university professors, researchers, or some kind of specialist in particular content areas (e.g., criminology, gerontology, gender studies, race and ethnic relations, etc.). In the long run, this hesitancy of labeling ourselves as sociologists is counter productive--it further reduces our identity and legitimacy in the marketplace. Seldom do you hear of psychologists, economists, physicians, or lawyers who are reluctant to identify themselves as such. We need to take pride in our profession, what we are able to offer, and the utility of our knowledge and skills. We must realize that if we do not sell ourselves, no one else will. (The Useful Sociologist, Society for Applied Sociology, Vol. 16, Summer, 1995.)

In conclusion, Nadia has sought sociological opportunity in a variety of contexts. But she is not easily compartmentalized. And, she recommends strongly that those coming into the profession be similarly oriented. Among other things Nadia seeks a transformation of sociology as a discipline. Entrepreneurship is one means. Therefore, to students Nadia says, "By all means take the opportunity of internships. See how the world actually works. By doing so you begin to understand just how your discipline works."

NOTE:

For more information important to this career, see the following chapters in *Sociology: A Down to Earth Approach,* by James M. Henslin:

24.

CAREERS IN SOCIOLOGY-
THE FIRST JOB

As most of us trek through college, we operate under some rather paradoxical notions regarding our studies, and the potential those studies have for a career. Many of us are bombarded by questions, usually from well-meaning family and friends, regarding what we are going to "do" once we graduate. At the same time, we are told that college is a time to explore our interests, and that something called "general ed" is good for us, even if we cannot somehow divine the relationship between a class in fine arts and making a living after graduation. Rene, now just one year removed from graduation, was probably typical in this regard. "My first thoughts of career grandeur, as I began my higher education, consisted of vague thoughts of medicine and travel. But first semester physics proved that was not the path for me. In retrospect, I really hadn't given much thought to an actual career. At that time I had no concept of how to shape my experiences towards a particular goal." Even when we do have some specificity, it is likely that our ideas, and our ideals will undergo substantial revision as a function of the undergraduate experience. This is not to say that no freshmen have such clear ideas. Only that most do not, and the rest often change their minds. Reflecting back on those early days, and the connection to career, Rene offers the following assessment: "Career objective? What's that? Do I need one of those? Is it going to be on the test? I hadn't a clue what I wanted to do!"

However, with time, with experience, with friends and family making suggestions, and with faculty eager to impart, or simply to collect majors, most students begin to make some kind of sense out of their interests and curiosities. This does not mean that any connection is yet made to a career. Only that we do begin to coalesce our thinking and experiences. And, we do get to the point of being able to say something about our studies, and even perhaps about what we are considering post graduation. Rene's case reflects this norm. "Sociology had always impressed me as a word that sounded very intellectual and esoteric. It was something that not very many people specialized in, and for that reason it was appealing to me. Fortunately it manifested other high points as well, along the way. Since high school, I had been looking forward to taking a sociology class, just to find out what this whole 'people study' business was about. I was pleasantly surprised, and even though the introductory course was mandatory, I found myself almost subconsciously signing up for anthropology, the social theory, and on and on...until I realized I wasn't too far off from a major."

This is not to say that Rene did not have other interests, or that her path into and through sociology was in any way straightforward. According to Rene, "I had wandered around through about six different majors in the course of two years…all of which totally surprised me. I never would have guessed I'd be signing on as a religion/philosophy major, or a business and modern languages degree candidate. But through this academic odyssey, one thing stayed the same, and that was sociology. I enjoyed my classes, and thanks to my professor's advice, felt confident that I could couple sociology with any other major, and still graduate on time with a healthy, well-rounded education. Finally, after realizing I was in love with literature, I settled on English as my second major…much to my mother's chagrin. She was slightly unsettled that I now had TWO 'worthless' majors. Fortunately, I was armed with the ammunition that she herself opted for the BA in French! Other than her eye-rolling and heavy sighing whenever she had to tell someone what I was studying, no one really objected to the degrees I had chosen to pursue."

Beyond figuring out the major, the inevitable questions arise regarding plans. But these plans, like much of the rest of the undergraduate experience, are emergent functions. That means it is constantly unfolding, sometimes clearly, and sometimes not. Some look back on these years as times of discovery. That is not meant to sound cliché, but to actually describe an important process. As Rene recalls: "During those college experiences I discovered that I loved to travel. Not just travel, but LIVE abroad. I had suspected that I might. My time in the Philippines was confirmation of that. I discovered that I had somewhat of a gift for adapting to new situations and making others comfortable in the midst of abundant cultural differences. So, I knew for certain that after graduation I wanted to live abroad. But that was all I knew. My sociological inclinations kept me fascinated with people, and I knew I needed to get out and see some more."

If the process of discovery is to be genuine, then it is imperative that you be open to the actual process. Many of us have professed dislike for something with which we have had no experience. This does not mean that you have to experience falling off a cliff for yourself in order to know something about the experience. However, wiser ones among us will usually ask us how we know we don't like something that we have never even considered, let alone tried. Rene was set on having the experiences, and often sought out advice and opinion about what she should, or might do. And, there are always significant others around with various agendas. In some cases, the agenda will say that you should not explore, that you should not step outside the prescribed limits. Rene often pushed those limits. According to Rene: "I had looked into different possibilities of fleeing my homeland for the joys, wonders, and trials of other cultures. Countless organizations exist to help wanderlust youths such as myself, make themselves useful abroad." But possible does not necessarily equal probable. In fact, even when your vision begins to come into focus, there is typically much more to be done, and experienced. According to Rene, "I applied for a scholarship which would allow me to study in Sierra Leone, I looked into the Peace Corps, I applied through two different organizations to teach English in Eastern Europe, and I even tried to get a job at an orphanage in Morocco. But almost all of these options fell through." So, what to do? In Rene's frame of mind, "...as morning dawned, peaceful and serene over our campus spotted with nervous graduation candidates, mortarboards sitting crooked or backwards on their heads, waiting for the umbilical cord to be cut...I had no plans for my future."

Well, yes and no. No, Rene did not have a job. But that does not mean that the education was now somehow irrelevant. What is required is the larger picture, though admittedly, that is not easy to see when Mom is "...rolling her eyes and sighing heavily." However, one year out, Rene does see that larger picture:

"Throughout college, graduation seemed like this culmination point that would never really come, so there was no need to worry too excessively about it...until all of a sudden I woke up one morning in March of my senior year and realized I had missed the deadline to order a cap and gown. Then I realized that this was it! This was my only chance. My graduation wasn't going to happen twice. I couldn't put it off...like I'd been putting off all my sociology seminar coursework. It was at about this same time that I woke up to the fact that even though I had two majors, I had no guarantee of a job, much less a career (especially the majors I had chosen). Suddenly my mother's chagrin was becoming a little more understandable. So, at that point I began to feel a little unprepared for this great world that was about to open up before me."

"However, as I began to update my CV, fill out applications for particular overseas fellowships and the Peace Corps, and write up some summaries of my college career, I noticed that I actually had quite a wealth of valuable experiences which, coupled with my two useless degrees, might actually land me some part-time temp work somewhere! In all seriousness, my academic advisor (incidentally my primary sociology professor) had encouraged me at every step along the way to take advantage of all kinds of interesting opportunities. He told me that they didn't have to 'make sense,' or fit in with my areas of studying. Basically, he just encouraged me to take any opportunity that appealed to me and run with it! And in looking back, I found that I had done just that. In those four years at college, I had participated in a play (something I had never done before), sung in the choir, edited the student newspaper, counseled incoming freshmen, lived in inner-city Chicago for a month, worked in a crisis pregnancy center, took part in a three-week seminar on the sociology of religion at the University of Notre Dame, and traveled to the Philippines as a teacher/volunteer. In addition, I spent my summers doing everything from waiting tables to assisting in the physical therapy ward at the hospital to writing news copy for a radio station, to piecing together portfolios at a financial advisory firm, to working at a water theme park. Each different piece of my four years showed me things about myself: things I liked to do, things for which I had no talent, things I wouldn't want to do for the rest of my life, things I thought were easy, but were in truth quite difficult. So, while I never consciously thought about my post-graduation job or career until that morning in March, I realized I had been doing something about it for the past four years."

While certainly a brave spin on the circumstances, the fact remained, Rene did not have a job, nor did she have reasonably viable prospects at the time of graduation. There were still a number of outstanding applications, but nothing remotely certain. "But amazingly enough, my sociology degree and I managed to get ourselves employed within one week of graduation! A neighbor whose children I had both babysat and taught piano for many years heard of a temporary opening in the government department with which he shared office space. Because of a conversation we had had the previous Christmas regarding my particular interests in international issues of all sorts, he immediately thought of me and recommended me for the position. Thus, three days after I arrived home from college I interviewed at the U.S. Department of Commerce, U.S. Export Assistance Center, and was gainfully employed by the end of the month."

We have all kinds of ways of interpreting what had just happened to Rene. Some would say "dumb luck," others would say providence. Few would say that Rene had actually produced the opportunity. Rene called it, "...a blow to the head! A pitch I never saw coming! How in the world did I end up in a government office, talking to [local] business owners about exporting their products overseas? I was still trying to figure out how to get to Turkey to teach English when I found myself researching the market for portable air conditioning units in Egypt (which, incidentally, is quite good). This position was contracted for eight months and during that time, my brain was pumped full of all sorts of information on economics, market research and political situations in every country imaginable, thus opening my eyes to the realm of global economics...a topic which had been tickling the back of my brain for a while."

One might reasonably ask, how was Rene qualified for such work? Rene asked the same: "What WAS I doing in the Department of Commerce with no business background whatsoever?" Others also asked, or at least wondered. According to Rene, "I usually got a good laugh out of colleagues...when they asked what I had studied. The answer, sociology and English, without fail was met with raised eyebrows or outright guffaws...except by the man who hired me, and that's what counts. But soon enough, I discovered that it would be very difficult to do this job WITHOUT some sort of sociological background! Sociology helped me to see the bigger picture and figure out where all the pieces and players fit in. Business and commerce are vital components to any society. They dictate the economy and thus often dictate the standard of living and the very culture itself. Thus, trying to understand all the implications of Mr. Johnny

Parker, who has never left Cleburne, TX, but wants to sell horse saddles to Mr. Almhed Habib in Saudi Arabia, takes a stretch of the imagination and an understanding of how to connect these two individuals through extensive people networks and subtle cultural education. Also, I discovered that small business owners have a little subculture unto themselves. I learned to quickly identify whether a company had good export potential just by different behavior patterns in the individuals in charge, or by the way the company was structured."

As is often the case, when we look back, we begin to see pathways and connections which were not even visible earlier. Such is the "magic" of networking. If you fail to get the word out, then opportunities cannot find you. We so often think of our careers as this linear function that is dependent on our efforts and our merit. Sometimes it does work that way. But more often it does not. This is not to say our preparations are irrelevant. Reread Rene's statement above to that effect. Rather, it is to say that by intentionally making and establishing connections, all kinds of connections, you are more likely to be in a position to be "found" by opportunity. We have a saying about opportunity "knocking." To many of us that seems just a bit too mystical. But for the person unprepared opportunity never seems to knock. Think about it.

Rene's saga, however, was only just beginning. "Two months into this new job, I got a phone call from a faculty couple who had taught at my college. They were packing their bags for Africa where he would take up the country director's position for an agricultural development NGO (non-governmental organization) in Mozambique. She would be coordinating a study-abroad program for the college students from my alma mater, also in Mozambique. Knowing me and my desires for working overseas in some sort of 'social' capacity, they invited me (just one week before they boarded their plane) to join them as a volunteer. My first thought was, NO WAY! I was still holding out for Turkey, and I honestly couldn't think of one good reason why anyone would go to Mozambique. Despite my internationally-focused job, I still had to check a globe to figure out exactly where Mozambique was. However, one week and a lot of soul-searching later, I phoned them back and told them to count me in. What eventually persuaded me to scrap my visions of Turkish grandeur was...the realization that I'm not an English teacher. I was simply using that as a way to get to another country, but it's not something I'm particularly good at, or enjoy. This offer to work with community development projects in rural Mozambique by writing up reports and publicity about those projects, and the opportunity to serve as a guide/counselor/translator for a group of twenty American college students, and facilitate their cultural adaptation and understanding...That was a better match for my abilities and desires. That made me excited."

As with the Department of Commerce, it can reasonably be asked, in what ways was Rene qualified? According to Rene, "My current position on Mozambique seems to make a little more sense sociologically, since one of my main tasks is to help twenty American students adjust culturally to the society in which they temporarily live. It is often much easier to make sociological observations on a society which is foreign. Thus, as I am required to write reports for Food for the Hungry, International, I am practically forced to make observations about Mozambican communities, ask questions, and find answers. In this process I constantly find myself on the edge, confronting new socially constructed realities, and loads of discomfort and anomic stress for myself! I encounter systems that work differently from my own, and I am forced to examine both sides to understand why Mozambicans do the things the do, as well as why Americans do the things they do."

For many, sociology seems to be the study of the exceptional rather than the normal. In part, this is due to the fact the discipline causes us to see the normal in different ways. This is precisely how Rene sees the benefit of sociology to her emerging role. "As I have already mentioned, the greatest benefit I have from by background in sociology is that it helps me see the big picture. I can work from day to day with individual people, become friends with them, get frustrated with them, talk to them. But because of sociology, I can look past that individual contact to a larger system of which they are a part. And, I can step back and look at the larger system of which I am a part. Then I can compare the two systems, and look for ways to try and bring them together. Or, at the very least, I can gain a better understanding of that individual's behavior or response as a manifestation of their societal and cultural influences. Often I can even predict the outcome of certain situations. Sociology reminds me to take a lot of different pieces: history, tradition politics, geography, religion, and fit them together as a frame around the people I look at face to face every day."

Taken out of the context of time, one might think Rene has been at this for quite a while. In fact, she graduated only a little over a year ago. So much packed into so very little time. Rene has not stood still, and has developed perspectives which will stand her in good stead in whatever she does. Her exclamation, "I soon discovered that it would be very difficult to do this job WITHOUT some sort of sociological background!" is instructive. But just one year out, what does Rene now think of her options? "My position here (Mozambique) is only temporary, and since it's voluntary work, my job security goes hand in hand with the amount of money that comes in from supporters. So, already people are asking me, 'What next?'" Graduate school is a definite step, but maybe not the next step. I would like to continue studies either in international communication, or economic development...something along those lines. My dream is to be able to write about people, the perfect combination of my two worthless degrees. It would seem too good to be true if someday I could just write about all my experiences, be a voice from one culture to another, and get paid for it. But for now, I'm looking forward to returning to the States to perhaps do some work with refugee relocation organizations. I'd like to work on the flip side of what I'm doing now, and help those people who find themselves in a sociological, culture shock nightmare, with no option of going home. I'd like to make them feel comfortable in my own society. Another tentative plan is to take the Foreign Service exam and join up with the State Department. Then, after completing my graduate work, I'd like to move overseas again, either in a governmental capacity, or again with a development agency."

As mentioned just above, Rene has already packed much into her young life, and she is already well on her way to figuring out the next steps. Some of you may find this interesting, or even alluring. And, some may find it just too much to consider! But, Rene does have a story to tell, and there are lessons to be learned. So, in retrospect, what advice would Rene give to the undergraduate, just starting out? "Honestly, I'd say don't worry about a career. Unless you know for certain what you want to do for the rest of your life, don't worry about it. Take it one step at a time. Do what you like doing, NOW. Carpe diem, if you will. In general, it's never safe to think more than one or two steps ahead, because chances are you'll change before you get there anyway! The best thing you can do while still in college is, ANYTHING that you haven't done before. Do something you're afraid to do. You'll stretch yourself and perhaps make discoveries which will give you direction for your next step. If at all possible, take a semester to study abroad. Nothing will change you more, and no matter what your degree, you can integrate your experiences into your education. It also makes you more marketable to any employer in this rapidly shrinking world. In addition, any sociology class you take, even if you only take one, will benefit you throughout your life…simply because you learn to pay attention. You learn to think about the things that no one else things about. You learn to ask questions about the everyday patterns that no one else asks about. This makes you astute, observant, and one step ahead of everybody else!"

25.

CAREERS IN SOCIOLOGY
RESEARCH IN CRIMINAL JUSTICE

Linda Swanson will say that her pathway to and through sociology, and finally to the career she has begun, is just not typical. Linda, with a master's degree in sociology, works as a researcher for a state agency charged with producing studies on a variety of criminal trends. Recent studies have focused on sex offenders and drunk driving by females. According to Linda, "I really do find doing research interesting. I like discovering the patterns and digging into the subject. If you are curious, and you have the skills, then research can be very rewarding. I like it when I am able to figure out just what is happening. While we have no real latitude on what we study, you always have to exercise your judgment in terms of how you conduct that study." For this Linda is compensated reasonably well, at about $55,000 per year. "But I'm thinking about returning to graduate school sometime and working on my doctorate. There are other things I'd like to do." Thus far, Linda's career developments seem rather normal, despite her statements to the contrary.

What seems rather unusual is that Linda spent three-plus years studying for a degree in pharmacy. "You see, while I was still in high school my mother mentioned to me that a classmate of mine was going to get a degree in pharmacy. She seemed to think it was quite a good idea. A degree in pharmacy was a five-year program, and then you are through. At that time the economy was not going so well, and it seemed to me that many people were having a difficult time getting a job, and a degree in pharmacy seemed practical, more secure. It really wasn't the case that being a pharmacist was something I'd dreamed of doing. My only real connection was that I had always liked math and science, and I had done well enough in them to make me think I could probably handle pharmacy. So, that's what I decided to do. Actually, looking back, it seems kind of weird, what my thinking was. I did have some interest in psychology, but that just did not seem nearly as certain or definite. I knew that if I went that route that I'd have to go on for a graduate degree, and I just wasn't ready to make that commitment. It's funny though, because I ended up getting a graduate degree, and am even considering the doctorate."

While still studying pharmacy, Linda did work as an intern, and she was able to observe, up close, the life and work of the pharmacist. And, she did not really like what she was seeing. "Where I was working, the pharmacists were working twelve-hour shifts, three days on and two days off. That seemed like a grind. But, even more than that, they basically count pills. That's it! It was really monotonous. When you add this to the stress of the major, particularly studying for major exams, I found that I just did not want to do it. I did not want to go through the stress of the studies, only to then have a career that was so uninteresting to me. In fact, I recall some of the other students in my dorm who were majoring in psychology or philosophy, and the things they were studying were just so interesting. I was even kind of jealous of them, because of the kinds of classes they were able to take. When I look back, I was not really on a path for success, either in class or in work. I felt as if I was just getting older and older, and going nowhere. Finally, I just had to decide that pharmacy was not for me."

After deciding that pharmacy was not her future, Linda left school, moved back home, and took classes at a nearby state school in order to redirect her studies. "I had always been motivated by helping others, and had once thought about social work. That was before the practicality of pharmacy took hold. So, I thought perhaps about going in that direction now." So, she began taking courses in psychology and sociology, before transferring again to a four-year school. While interested in social work, Linda was not so sure she was interested in the "nitty-gritty" kind of social work. Plus, she began developing more interest in psychology and social psychology. "Basically, for a year I studied in psychology and social psychology, but then discovered that with just a couple of more courses I could get a double major in psychology and sociology. So, I decided to finish the sociology major as well. Sociology was really something I did at the very end of my undergraduate studies, not at all intending to go that route. Really, I just kind of fell into it."

However, while Linda had not intended sociology, there were parts of it that she found quite interesting. Among other things, her priorities were changing. She was becoming more committed to people, and to intrinsic values. The courses she was taking challenged her in this way. They also challenged her to think. "In pharmacy I was just learning what others were telling me. I was just so much content. In sociology and psychology I was challenged to think. I was expected to think, to have an idea and to be able to defend it. I was beginning to discover the underlying reasons for why things happen in society, and I was developing skills for studying that. I found that all very attractive. In fact, that opened up many other areas of study to me, areas that I just had not even considered before. So, I was just very interested in learning as much as I could about as many different things as I could. It was also such a great relief from the studies in pharmacy. It was just so much fun, learning, that I did not really even give any thought to the career implications of my choices. I just knew by then that I'd have to go on for my master's, if I were to get any kind of job, so I just did not worry much about it as an undergraduate." To this end, Linda's parents were supportive, even though it was partly at their suggestion originally, that she pursue pharmacy. Then, in her last undergraduate semester, one of her advisors told her that there was a graduate course being offered, and that she could enroll in that if she wanted.

Linda felt that in order to produce options for eventual employment, she needed to go on to graduate school, and so she took the suggestion to get a jump on her graduate classes now. "I thought it was a really good opportunity. But, at the same time, I had to be doing something, either getting a job or continuing in school. Actually, I was a bit panicky about my circumstances. Staying in school gave me direction. Plus, I liked what I was studying." Because of the changes Linda had made in her undergraduate tracks, she had needed to take an extra semester to finish her bachelor's degree. So, she went from being an undergraduate in December to being a graduate student in January. However, Linda was not especially clear about how to turn this education into a job, let alone a career. "In my first semester (the spring semester) I just took classes that were interesting. But in the fall it kind of hit me, I needed a plan if graduate school was going to work for me. What that meant was to take classes that were more practical, the skills classes. So, I began taking more and more classes in research, or with research components. I was also gearing up on statistics, SPSS, and other related skills. One of the more interesting things about taking these classes is that there were students in them from all different fields and parts of the world. Many of them had already begun careers, and were going to grad school while still working. I learned from them more about myself, what I wanted to do, and, more importantly, what I wanted to be. Research seemed to fit my needs in this regard."

During her graduate studies, Linda not only took classes, but took a research assistantship with one of the graduate faculty. "That was really one of the best things I did. I learned so much about how to conduct research, how to manage all the details, and began understanding how to make the important decisions within the research design. I have to say that I really liked it. I liked working with the data and finding the patterns in various populations. Plus, I knew I was getting something very practical." Critical to all this was Linda's relationship with the faculty in her department. Her advisor and the faculty person whom she served as a research assistant provided invaluable assistance and advice all throughout Linda's studies. By age 24, Linda then had the graduate degree that she had once thought would take too long to earn, and for which she was uncertain regarding employment prospects. She had accomplished the opposite of her initial intentions.

With her Master's in hand, Linda felt strongly that it was time to go to work. She had considered staying on for her Ph.D., but was at a stage of her life where work was more important. "All my friends not in this program had jobs, and here I was still in school. On the one hand I enjoyed school, but I had a need to be more practical." So, Linda began the job search. "Basically, I made application to every kind of research position I could find. I was looking in the paper, on-line, and in any source for job ads. I looked for those positions that needed research skills, but also looked at social work related jobs as well, just to cover all bases. If some organization just needed data management, such as SPSS, I applied. I was always carrying around this portfolio of my search." Beginning around mid-May, Linda began this search, and within about a month and a half she had a job. How did this happen so quickly? According to Linda, "As I was finishing my research assistant work, I was actually doing some training of the new graduate student doing that work. While at work, one of the faculty inquired about my job search, and ended up suggesting that I call this department (the government department where she now works). So I did, and in a day I had an interview! It really happened very quickly."

For the past three years, Linda has participated in a number of studies on data coming out of the state's court system. Based on arraignments in courts, Linda's department tracks a variety of crime patterns, and manages two annual reports on court statistics. Her individual projects run from small to large data sets, specific studies, and annual reports based on data management. The results of each report are then made available to the authorizing department or party, and are also released to the public. Ultimately, the public are the consumers of the research done by Linda and her colleagues. While a study may be specific, Linda will nonetheless "...gather everything I can about the topic. When you are looking for patterns or trends in the data, you never know just what might be the most significant variables. If you limit yourself to certain preconceived notions, then you are likely to miss whole trends." Interestingly, even though Linda's research is nearly always court and crime based, her studies in graduate schools were not in criminal justice. When asked how can she do research in such an area, Linda replies, "The basics of research are applicable to all subject matter. Besides, I have learned how to adapt to the needs of each project. It is the challenge of figuring things out that I find most appealing."

Linda has been motivated by a number of interests and agendas, both hers and others. She has both undergraduate and graduate degrees, and she has a job for which she is prepared and skilled. She likes research, and feels she is good at it. She makes a decent salary and likes her colleagues. Yet, according to Linda, "I just cannot see myself doing this for the rest of my life. I'm thinking seriously about returning to graduate school for my Ph.D., though I do not know just now what that will be in, or just what I want to do with it. I guess that sounds kind of funny, and I'll probably look back on this time, say five years from now, and see how the decisions I make now will impact the rest of my life and career." So, based on her own experiences, what would Linda have to say to the undergraduate today? "I'd say that while the social sciences generally, and sociology in particular, are valuable areas of study, you have to work at making them practical. I think that my best advice would be that students consider double-majoring, or something like that. This way you can combine the practicality of something like business, with the general perspective and tools of sociology. You also need a clear understanding of what a particular profession or career entails and will require of you. So much of what people think will be part of a job or career just does not turn out. My opinion is that too many of us have skewed ideas about what will really be required." Not bad advice from one who has done the about-faces in her life and career, but who has also demonstrated the kind of vision, determination, and habits to make it work.

26.

CAREERS IN SOCIOLOGY-
SPORTS AND HIGHER EDUCATION

His name is Sam Hollister, age 46. He recently accepted a position in higher education administration, as academic dean, after nearly 25 years in the classroom. In some respects, Sam's career developed in a fairly typical manner. He was the son of an academic, earned an undergraduate degree, and took a scholarship to graduate school. Near the end of his graduate studies, Sam accepted an offer to return to his alma mater where he taught for the next seventeen years, before accepting an offer to become an academic dean. According to Sam, "When you look at it this way my career seems rather simple and straightforward. I'm not sure that many would aspire to it. On the other hand, I cannot think of anything for which I would trade what I have experienced." Like many pictures, you really have to dig beneath the surface in order to more fully understand. That is certainly the case with Sam.

"Heading into college, I probably identified more with athletics that I did with academics. Not that I was 'anything to write home about' as far as athletics, but it was through sport that I had my identity. I had attended three high schools in one three-year stretch, and sport was the means by which I carved out my niche, acquired friends, became someone..." Academically, Sam was sound as a student. "I was bright enough to often get by without my best effort. At the same time, I was always interested in taking on extra projects, whether it was science fairs or music competitions. I had my interests, though they were not always in line with the traditional subjects being offered in school."

Upon graduation from high school, Sam was still as much motivated by his connection to sport as to academics and career. So, the day after graduation, he left home, really for the first time, and spent the summer coaching tennis at a resort in the far west. "I have to admit to being rather impressed with my circumstances, and especially the fact that I was a part of it. Well-known people came to our resort, I got to meet them, and work with them. And, I had something that they all wanted, skill in tennis. Besides the daily lessons, we also put on exhibitions with crowds of people gathered to see just how tennis was to be played. It was pretty heady stuff for a seventeen-year-old. However, I also knew that I was not the best at tennis among my peers at the resort, and that I would eventually have to give serious consideration to just what I wanted to do with my life after tennis."

While tennis skill, and learning the details of how to teach the sport, were certainly acquired, it was actually in the development of people skills that Sam really benefited from that first summer as a teaching pro. "The director of the resort was a real stickler about how we related to the people who came through our program. For example, he made it clear that while we did give tennis lessons, 90% or more of the people that came would not really make any progress in their tennis. Instead, what they really wanted was the attention that we as coaches gave to them for a week or a weekend. We typically had 140 people come through our program every week, and we had to figure out how best to relate to each and every one. In fact, we were simply required to be able to call each of those 140 people by name on the second meeting with any one of them! I thought that would be impossible when I first started out, but soon found ways to recall names. I was amazed at how important that was, and how impressive it was to our students. And, it did make a difference. I also learned some important lessons regarding social roles. Here I was, seventeen years old, and I was in a position to tell some CEO that he had a lousy backhand. But, no matter how lousy it was, I could not say so. In fact, I found that it was difficult to tell any such person what he or she ought to do with their strokes. Instead, I learned to present options to such people, and then I let them decide how to proceed. Of course, I controlled to some extent those options, but I created a situation in which they still had a semblance of control. While they may not have always made the optimum choice, it was their choice, nonetheless, and they typically made some progress at the very least." Altogether, Sam spent about six summers giving lessons.

After that first summer, Sam returned and attended his hometown college, the same college where various members of his immediate and extended family had attended. It was comfortable. But, there was not, as yet, any specific academic motive. Sam had had interests in biology and anthropology, but these did not coincide with the directions those disciplines were taking at that college at that time. "Basically, I just began by taking courses in the general education curriculum. I had managed to test out of some basic courses, and even took a couple of advanced courses, but I got in over my head, at least as far as my interests were concerned, pretty quickly. In my second semester, however, I took a course that came strongly recommended by some faculty, and students as well. It was introductory sociology. While I found the subject matter interesting, I found the professor substantially more interesting. I liked the way he conducted class, and he was always willing to engage and challenge students, and the ideas we thought we had. I especially liked the way he dealt with some of the upper classmen who were just trying to finish out their undergraduate degrees with a final required course or two. He just would not let them off the hook. He made them defend their ideas, and he would not let them just hide in class. They were going to get something out of class, whether they wanted to or not!"

At the conclusion of that introductory class, Sam had completed his first piece of research, elementary though it was. In many ways, it was like the project work he had done in high school. "I liked the feel of being able to set my own course and make my own case. I like the debate." At the end of that first course, the professor suggested that I might want to take anthropology in the fall. "I did not know at that time that anthropology was a part of that particular department's curriculum for majors in sociology. I just knew that I was interested in it, and it held the same kind of opportunity for research, debate, and discovering more about people."

Over the next couple of years, Sam continued taking courses in the sociology department, playing tennis on the college team, and teaching in the summers. "What I found was that in various ways what I was learning in class fit quite well with what I was experiencing. Being part of a team was full of interesting dynamics. Tennis, in particular, required that I think my way through matches, as much as simply play my way through. If one strategy did not work, then something else had to be tried, and nearly immediately. There are no substitutions in tennis. If you are taking lumps in a match, then you just had to take them, unless you could figure something out. The same could be said for teaching tennis to all kinds of people over the summers. And, I was learning more and more about how people functioned in the classes I was taking. But I still had no clear career objective."

Around the first of his junior year, members of Sam's family and faculty in the sociology department began to make suggestions as to what he might do with himself after graduation. "Both my father and grandfather began talking about law, and encouraged me to look into that possibility. In fact, my grandfather told me that he had had such an interest at one point in his life, and in some respects still did. I also brought this up with the one faculty member in sociology who was really serving as my mentor, even though I had not declared sociology as a major. Interestingly, he also had had such an interest in law. But, he told me that I needed to make sure I do first things first, and that meant declaring a major and getting on with a degree. He also promised me that he'd help promote my developing interest in law." In his senior year, this promise played out in a recommendation by his professor of a kind of internship with a local lawyer. "That was a really heady experience for me. I got to satisfy both my developing interest in law, along with my new research skills in sociology. I was even called to testify in a case in which my research was influential. Interestingly, my advisor in sociology was called in for the prosecution on that case, basically to question the validity of my work. As it turned out, we prevailed. I recall being quite full of myself at the time."

Sam was also working on a senior project. "Again, it was something that I got to choose, design, debate, and defend. And, I was asked to come to some of the undergraduate classes, such as intro and research methods, and present what I was doing. I enjoyed it, more than I though I would." Up to that time, Sam had submitted applications to law school, but he decided to submit one to graduate school as well. "I was thinking, just in case I don't get into law school, at least I could go to grad school, though I really did not know much if anything about it. While I had seemed to be sure of where I was going with my education, I was now not so sure. But this I did know, I needed options. Applying to both law and grad school made sense."

In the spring of his senior year, Sam was accepted to both law and graduate school. Now he had to choose. "It really was a difficult choice, in terms of my interests. I enjoyed both my internship in the law office, and my senior project. I would have to say, however, that a very pragmatic consideration began to take hold of my decision. I was getting married right after graduation, and my fiancée already had a teaching job in the vicinity of the university where I'd applied for graduate studies in sociology. Plus, I'd earned a scholarship. It seemed, in light of all that, a rather easy decision to stick with sociology." After getting married, and after a final summer of resort tennis, Sam started graduate studies in sociology.

"I have to admit that initially the idea, and even the experience of grad school, was a bit overwhelming. I recall one fellow student asking me, what kind of sociologist I was? I did not even know there were kinds! Actually, I just did not even understand the question. But what I did find out was that success in graduate school relied largely on two factors. One, clearly assessing the lay of the land, particularly the faculty in the department, and two, taking the initiative. While I did not initially know what kind of sociologist I was, I did know how to pose a research question and how to gather data that mattered. In many respects, these were the same skills I'd learned while playing and teaching tennis. If you cannot figure out the situation you are presently in, assessment, then you cannot possibly figure a way forward, or even out. In fact, it is as important to know the right question as it is to know the right answer. It's the question that will lead you to the answer. Further, you must be absolutely honest with yourself and acknowledge when it is that you don't know something! More people fail by overreaching, in my opinion, than by simply not being able to succeed."

Graduate school was both a tremendous challenge, and a tremendous boost to Sam's sense of himself, and where he might be going. But the Ph.D. did not simply lay out for him an unambiguous path to a career. There was a basic assumption that he would be going into an academic setting and teach. He had learned much about teaching, primarily through trial and error, "...and the advice of my elementary school teacher wife!" But Sam's research had nearly all been what the discipline would come to call as applied. "I'd worked with social action groups, investigated the inner workings of a legislature, served in a state department of corrections, documented organizational change in a major multinational, and even consulted with some small businesses, in addition to the basic teaching opportunities I'd had in the area. I liked teaching, but I also liked the projects, just as I always had."

At the conclusion of his graduate studies, Sam had already secured a teaching position in one of the new proprietary institutions that were gaining a foothold in higher education at that time. "The pay was excellent, but there just was no room to maneuver. It was obvious that I was more of an assembly line teacher. While that job met an immediate need, specifically financially, it did not meet my growing interests in how my discipline, how sociology, could be applied to a variety of different settings and problems. My work in organizational development was particularly interesting, though nearly any circumstance undergoing change I found fascinating." Within a year, Sam's undergraduate alma mater called, and he was offered a position as a replacement for the very professor who had served as his mentor years before.

"In some respects I felt just like I did at the start of any new experience or challenge. I found the circumstance a bit overwhelming. But, I also found that I had been prepared, not for specific functions or activities, but prepared to adapt, to figure out what to do next." It was also the case that the college had begun going through some very difficult fiscal times. "I remember the dean calling me in at the start of the second semester and telling me to make sure my resume was in order. Things were getting worse, not better, and it may be the case that I'd have to look elsewhere for work in the fall. I have to admit, that was a bit of a shock. But it also caused me to refocus my efforts. While teaching was my primary responsibility, I came to understand that I had to create a department, not just maintain. It was the same old story, just different actors and settings."

Over the course of the next seventeen years, Sam focused his energies on building an undergraduate program of sociology. However, this would prove impossible to do if the spectrum of efforts had been narrowed specifically to sociology. "One of the strengths of the discipline is that it forces you to always take a step or two back from the circumstance or challenge you are confronting. You understand that the larger picture is as important as the details. My research in multinational corporations certainly evidenced this to me. I often found people within an organization who simply had no idea, not just about what some other part of the organization was doing, but that it even existed. This often led to cross purposes in the efforts people were making. It's not unlike a football team in which a few critical players do not know what play is being called. I am not suggesting that having a larger picture necessarily leads to some kind of imperative to act on other parts, but that if you are in a position of trying to build or create something, it is necessary to know more than the immediate situation."

A particular focus of Sam's was to demonstrate that sociology was more than a requirement to be met. "It seemed to me that the relevance of sociology was both overlooked by most outside the discipline, and on the other hand, simply assumed by those within the discipline. The result was, when a student expressed interest in the field many faculty, like myself, were ill-equipped to provide meaningful answers." Sam began by turning the discipline of sociology upon itself, investigating what happened to students who had made the decision to study in the field. He also began looking at ways that the discipline could coordinate with other disciplines, such as business administration, education, and the sciences, as well as the other social sciences. What he found was that many more students found sociology at least somewhat interesting, but had no way of connecting that interest to their primary interest in some other field. One solution was to find ways for such students to experience their disciplinary interests in a variety of settings, including co-op's, internships, and cross-cultural settings, including study abroad. Typically, in such settings, students were forced to consider not only where they were and what they were doing, but they had to reflect on what was happening. It was opportunity for them to see the lessons of their disciplines, in particular the social relations of their work. For example, a student who was combining business with sociology found that the interpersonal relationships were just as critical as the latest technology or rules for accounting. The nursing student found that that there was much more to patient care than the biology or chemistry of the patient's illness. Such an applied focus actually centered sociology within the larger curriculum, rather than allowing it to remain in its often marginal position. Further, students began seeing the potential connections between their studies and initiating a career.

Throughout these years, Sam developed an ever-widening array of interests and applications. "Among other things, I continued to coach. And, I found that athletics was opening many, many doors that might have otherwise remained closed to me. At one point, my interests turned strongly to nations which were transitioning out of communism; in particular, China and the Soviet Union. In China, I joined a bike tour from Beijing to Shanghi. All along the way I was able to meet with local folks, those not typically available to tourists on a bus. I met with farmers, factory workers, school children, etc. I don't believe I would have had nearly as rich an experience otherwise. Further, I gained an important, ground-level perspective on economic reform in that land. In the Soviet Union, I accepted an assignment as a coach for the International Baseball Association. Shortly after baseball was introduced as an Olympic sport, it was necessary to send coaches around the world to offer instruction. For weeks I traveled all over the Soviet Union, but doing much more than simply coaching an American game. I was able to see, first hand, the emerging effects of glasnost and perestroika." Ultimately, such travels and experiences were reproduced in lessons and further travel opportunities for students.

According to Sam, the discipline of sociology was demonstrating itself to be most relevant, in a variety of settings. It was especially relevant regarding organization and social change. While there are many sub fields of sociology, organization and change are at the heart of the discipline, and not just in an academic or theoretic sense. Besides the classroom, Sam was involved in the advancement of the discipline via professional societies, was engaged as a consultant-evaluator for the accreditation of colleges and universities, and served on international development teams. "While I continued to be challenged by the work I was doing, and found it generally quite satisfying, I also found that I tended to respond better to the challenge of the project, than I did the routine. Twenty-five years of teaching, the last seventeen years in the same place, while rewarding, began to give way to thoughts of doing something else."

According to Sam, "I did what I had advised many, many students and others before. That is, I asked people who had been there before me for their insights and advice. I also asked them for recommendations. I don't mean the letter of recommendation in this case (though I did ask for those as well at the appropriate time). Instead, I asked them to think about my considerations, and to feel free to advise." The point of all this is that substantial changes in one's life ought to be approached like any other serious matter. "My life to that point had developed through an array of interests and efforts on my part, but mostly by way of the influence of others. My parents, wife, colleagues, professional contacts, etc. That is the same for all of us, though we often are not really paying close attention to such. It is often only when these significant others are no longer a part of our lives that we notice."

Eventually, Sam was presented with an opportunity to move into academic administration as an academic dean. He was in a small college, not unlike the one he had just served as a faculty member. "I would have to say that my feelings at the beginning were much like the feelings I've had at other beginnings; somewhat overwhelmed. I remember, clearly, the first day I reported to the office for work. After some small talk with the person who was to be my administrative assistant, I went into the office and sat down behind the desk. Then I remember wondering, almost out loud, 'Now what do I do?' In many ways I had thought I was ready for this. And, I think I was. But there were other ways in which I was not."

The intensity of the new role was perhaps the most significant impression. "People expected me to make decisions, right away. Yet I was feeling that I needed some time to adapt. The reality was, there was no time. I simply had to make do. I still had to adapt, but I had to do so on the run." On the run meant the following in Sam's first year. The president who had hired him resigned six weeks after Sam was hired. He was followed by an interim president, who had served as interim dean just prior to Sam taking the job. Seven months later the college's board of trustees hired a permanent president. So, Sam served three presidents in his first year as a dean, and a new dean at that. It was also the case that the college had been tasked by its accreditation association to undertake some substantial self-review and reform processes. So, rather than sit back and assess, with time, Sam and the faculty had to press on, regardless of the changes in the president's office. This meant discovering the lay of the land at this college, including its strengths and its challenges, while simultaneously trying to negotiate new terrain. According to Sam, "Engaging such weighty matters ran counter to all advice I'd been offered by those wiser than me. But I had no real choice." Finally, the substantive changes being experienced by this institution began to manifest themselves in personnel ways. By the end of Sam's first year, retirements and resignations had created vacancies in over a third of the full-time faculty positions. "While I had participated in the hiring of faculty, typically within my own department, I was in no way prepared for so many faculty from across the entire range of disciplines. That overwhelming feeling was once again near at hand."

As with all other such circumstances, Sam has stayed close to those who could offer wise counsel. Further, more often than not, Sam kept the bigger picture in mind, even as he was needing to make specific decisions in the present. "I cannot say that all of my decisions have been well made, or that the processes employed were the best, especially in hindsight. However, I feel confident in saying that my perspective, particularly my sociological perspective on organization and change, has served me well in terms of framing any issue, need, or challenge. Further, I know, clearly I think, what it is that I do not know. I may, and do, make mistakes, but they are rarely due to overreaching. Instead, I actively cultivate those who do know, who do have a specific interest or frame of reference, and I rely on their expertise. The college belongs to all of us, no matter how often we might think otherwise. And so, I continue to develop the essential and necessary relationships in order to accomplish our stated mission."

When asked to detail just what his job is, Sam hesitates. "It's not that I do not know what is involved; though there are times when I do not. But, it is difficult to state in a few words. Basically, I am responsible for keeping the institution's academic programming organized around, and making progress towards, its mission. This means, on the one hand, just spending informal time with faculty talking about program developments, while at other times it means official acts such as chairing meetings, making assignments, and hiring. At still other times it means activities as disparate as listening to student appeals, or authorizing expenditures for marketing of adult education programs. But in every case, it means working closely with a variety of others. According to Sam, "I don't like, and did not like while I was a faculty member, the concept of being managed. So, I consciously try to steer clear of managing others. On the other hand, I must stay close to a wide variety of significant others, often those who have competing agendas. Actually, I try to build a team, or several teams, so that we can get all done that must be done. However, I do understand that no matter how well settled things become, change is just around the corner. So, I always have one eye toward the future."

There is no particular conclusion here. Sam is in the middle of his career. In retrospect, Sam has been a teaching pro in tennis clubs and resorts, he has run the gamut of graduate school, he has taught in a variety of institutions, including overseas, he has consulted, he has developed new programs, and worked within the profession of his discipline. And, he is presently learning his new role as academic dean, though he would say that he certainly knows more about that role after one year than he could have imagined. It is the case, however, that Sam has demonstrated a willingness and a facility to adapt to new and different ways. Further, according to Sam, "It seems that as long as I manage to keep a proper perspective, that is, one which is not too full of self-importance, but rather keeps an eye on the larger picture, then I am largely able to keep making progress. You see, in coaching, losing was always a part of the equation. Dealing with failure was a necessity. If you could not deal with it, then there was no real sense in playing the game. I saw way too many people over the years who could deal with only one side of the game. And, even if I, or one of my players, did manage to win, there was always another round, another player ready to challenge. Perhaps the most telling example of this was what happened after I left my previous school for my present role. After seventeen years I guess I thought that I'd left some rather big shoes to fill. I was getting full of myself. Actually, it took them about three weeks to find replacements for all the roles I'd played. That was a good lesson for me, especially now. While I believe I've done a decent job thus far, I know that someone will eventually replace me. The sociologists are right about change!"

27.

CAREERS IN SOCIOLOGY-
SALES AND MID-CAREER CHANGE

At age 55, Jerry Grant is making a career change. It is not the first, though he hopes it is the last. At critical stages, significant others made suggestions, gave advice, and Jerry knew how and when to take advantage. You might say Jerry has become expert in the business of advice. He has given it to customers while settling insurance claims, to business owners while selling advertising for newspapers, and to students while teaching part time. He also knows how to take advice, as he has at several critical times in his life. There is a perspective in American culture that individuals choose their pathways and, therefore, somehow or another design their careers. To some extent that is true. But it is also true that we are products of our families, friends, prevailing culture, etc. Knowing this can allow us to actually begin to make those choices. Not knowing this can subject us to the choices of others, or simply the prevailing patterns of the community at large. The trick is discerning between the two. Jerry seems to have developed such a capacity. But changing a career at 55?

Jerry grew up as a military kid, moving often and having to adapt to a wide variety of settings. Settings as diverse as Oklahoma, Hawaii, France, and Massachusetts. As a young Black man growing up in the heart of the civil rights movement, Jerry developed further skills adjustment and acculturation. In many respects, these varied life experiences made sociology a natural area of study. However, while Jerry was gifted in the ways of people, sociology was not his first interest. "Actually," according to Jerry, "when I first started college, I really had no idea what I wanted to study or what I wanted to do. I had just graduated from high school in Hawaii, and through family and church connections I was going to be attending college in the Northeast. I remember the photo I sent in with my application. I was wearing a Hawaiian shirt and a lei around my neck. Then, here I am, on the East Coast, looking and presenting myself as a Polynesian from Hawaii. As I look back thirty-eight years, it was both funny and bizarre." While Jerry's choice of a college was faith related, his specific choice was not made until rather late in the game. "Because of this, I had not really given much thought as to what I might do while in college. I did have some interest in math and physics, however, and so I thought I would begin there and see where it might take me. I did have some dreams that tended towards aeronautical engineering, perhaps being a pilot, and maybe even an astronaut. But, my first calculus and physics grades came in, and they told me that while these were interesting fields of study, I was not achieving at the level necessary to be an astronaut. I really think that being an army brat, and moving so frequently, I just wasn't able to get the foundation I really needed in those fields. I was in four high schools in my sophomore year alone, and it took a toll on my academics. Nonetheless, I held on to the dream for two years, as my grades took a beating. It was only then that I decided I needed to move on to something else."

All of us, at one time or another, will confront the fact that some things will not work out. It may be a relationship, a skill, a job, or an area of study. This is not to say that there just is no future to be had, but that the particular future we had envisioned will be different. Being able to decide when enough is enough is far from failure, it is maturity. Jerry exhibited such maturity, and did so by listening carefully to the advice of significant others. "After I realized that math and science were not going to work out, I decided to turn towards philosophy. I enjoyed it, and my grades took a good turn for the better. But I was not yet performing at the level I believed I needed. I'd given philosophy a year, but I needed to move on. Interestingly, while I talked to a number of professors along the way, none were really helping me explore other areas of study. But one day I happened to be talking with the secretary to the college president. Her name was [Smith]. And she told me something about myself that, while I knew, I hadn't really honed in on. She said, 'You're a very good person who makes friends easily, and you seem to get along well with others. Have you ever thought about sociology? It might be something of interest to you.' So I thought about it, and I realized that I do like dealing with people. In fact, it seemed to me that this was one of my stronger qualities. And so, I decided that I should look into that." It was Jerry's junior year, and he was starting over.

In about a year and a half, Jerry started and completed a major in sociology. "I just began taking the courses, and I had to take a lot of them in order to finish. I found that I was really enjoying them. Each new course I took was more interesting and more challenging than the one before. I felt within myself that I was now at home, I was at peace, I was no longer struggling. More importantly, I was no longer questioning myself. I was more sure, more certain of myself. All these confirmed that sociology was the field for me." Jerry had indeed found his niche; he was happy with his studies, and did complete the requirements for the major in sociology. Because he had made the decision for sociology somewhat late, he needed an additional summer of coursework in order to finalize all requirements for graduation. As Jerry was nearing graduation, it became clear that, "I really had no idea what was going to happen next. In fact, I never had a discussion with any of my faculty regarding how to go on for a job, or just what to do. I really was on my own."

What happened next is that Jerry was again provided with some insightful advice. "You see, while I was in school I had been working part time, at several different places, to pay off my college education. I had worked for both an insurance company and an alarm installation company.

I learned quite a bit about work habits and responsibility. I had also learned how to work with people from all kinds of backgrounds and circumstances. I knew something about business. But I still had no idea as to just what I ought to do." It was the case, however, that his work experience had put Jerry in a position to access opportunities not otherwise available. In particular, the insurance company had a policy of trying to hire from the college students already working for them. "I was approached by the company and asked if I'd consider working full time after graduation. It sounded like a good opportunity, so I said yes."

As a part-time employee, Jerry's job had been to facilitate the claims process by interviewing clients who called in with claims. Basically phone work, Jerry would question claimants and/or the insured about their claim, gathering as much information as he could before passing the file on to a claims adjuster. The job Jerry took was that of a claim representative, building on the work he had already done. In many respects, it was a job well suited to a sociology degree. "It was all about understanding people, particularly people under stress. It was certainly more helpful than it would seem, on paper, to most. In order to work with people, under varying conditions, you have to find a way to connect. I had that ability to connect, and part of that came from sociology. For example, many of the people I came in contact with during the course of business were hostile in one way or another. They had a claim against my company. So I had to find a way to make them feel comfortable with the situation, and with me, in order to get the job done. Actually, if I did not do this well, I could just as easily make the client even more hostile. All I learned about human behavior in sociology was absolutely applicable, in very practical terms, from the collection of data to managing the interactions. It simply helped me do my job."

However, whatever else we know about life, things change. About two years into his work as a claims representative, the insurance industry went through a substantial change. According to Jerry, "Then came along this concept of no-fault insurance. What no-fault basically meant was that the previous system of fact-finding necessary to determine fault did not have to be done. No one really knew just what this meant for the industry, other than the process to finalizing claims would be shortened. That meant there would not be a need for as many claims representatives. So, I was told that as one of the last hired, I would be one of the first let go. It was purely a numbers game, and I was out of a job."

The next year was not easy. Jerry called it "foundering." "I was looking for work everywhere. I think I must have had sixty interviews in the year after loosing my job at the insurance company. That wasn't easy." The fact was, Jerry needed a job, and that made other kinds of choices more difficult to make. According to Jerry, "You see, while working in insurance I had begun to think that maybe I might go into the law. I was working with lawyers, the legal system, interviewing clients, writing reports, etc. It seemed like a fit. But there was something more. Coming

125.

out of my background in sociology, I had developed a strong interest in social justice. That, as much as anything, fueled my interest in law. I felt that whenever and wherever people in society were being taken advantage of, or were not able to defend themselves, I needed to be there, to somehow be their champion." Eventually, social justice was to become an even more substantial focus in Jerry's career, though after another stint with insurance.

Jerry eventually found another position in insurance, and worked in that field for another two years. However, according to Jerry, "I was coming to the conclusion that this was not what I really wanted to do. It was interesting, and I was successful, but I was not going anywhere."

In the 1970's, the Comprehensive Employment and Training Act produced what came to be called the CETA Program. While Jerry was still in insurance, a college friend contacted him and suggested that he might be well suited for CETA. According to Jerry, "He told me, [Jerry], you majored in sociology, and I'm going to need someone to do some social work. I need someone to counsel people in a variety of areas. Basically, we were providing education and training programs so that people who were currently unemployed, or underemployed, could get jobs. We wrote and administered curriculums in different kinds of areas, including some of the first training in computers. At other times, we set up training programs within existing businesses. During the training period, we provided stipends for the people in the program. Afterwards, we helped these people get and hold onto jobs." The work had a lot of variety to it. "We wrote curriculum for training ranging from computers, to auto body, to culinary arts, and secretarial skills. But my job went beyond the classroom. I was responsible for getting people into training, and staying in the program, counseling regarding problems on the job, and often with families. I had to help them figure out the various pressures in their lives, whether children or spouse, for example. The purpose was to keep them in training, and then help them find a job once they were done. I was involved in all aspects of the program. It was in this job that my interest in social justice was really satisfied. And, it was in this job that my sociological background really came into play. I understood social problems, and I was also motivated by a sense of social justice. My degree and my work were a perfect fit. It was very satisfying to take an individual who had no idea what they wanted to do, or no idea of their own interests, and help them assess themselves, discover interests, and then get the training necessary to be employable in their area of interest." An interesting contrast to Jerry's own circumstance at the end of his undergraduate education. According to Jerry, "One of the best results, personally, of this program has come in the years since I worked for CETA. I would be around town and someone who had been through our program would come up to me and tell me how much of a difference I had made in their lives. And they would thank me over and over, saying '...if you hadn't done that I don't know where I would be today. Now I have a career, my family is in order...' Hearing that is just a great feeling, a great feeling."

In the course of his work with CETA, Jerry had several different roles, roles which would turn up again and again as his career developed. Initially, Jerry served as a counselor, working case by case with clients of the program. Next, Jerry served as director of training, in which capacity he worked on a variety of curriculum matters. He both wrote curriculum and found curriculum partners in the community. So, he would negotiate with businesses to set up training programs, and, in turn, hire graduates of those programs. Later, Jerry was asked to manage public relations for the program. "It was important for both the public at large, and the participants as well, to know what was going on. There are always those who see a government program such as this as simply welfare. But when they could see the successes they would sometimes change their minds. This was important because our public was the source of new partners. At any one time we had from 1500 to 3000 participants in the program, and a staff of only forty. We also had to keep information flowing among participants, so I was responsible for things such as a newsletter. I worked with writers, artists, and served as the program's spokesman. I got to tell the public our story, and tried to assure them that, as a public agency, we were responsible with their tax dollars." In many respects, it was more evidence of the relevance of sociology to Jerry's work. He was having to adapt to all kinds of situations and people. It was these skills that mattered most.

Just as Jerry experienced a trend shift in private industry, the development of no-fault insurance, he also experienced a trend shift in a public agency. Governmental and societal changes in the late 1970's and early 1980's began to emphasize private, rather than public, initiative. This had a number of implications, both for CETA and for Jerry. Jerry had spent about seven years in CETA, working from entry level to spokesman for the program. At the same time, needs in his own life began to shift. He had a family to support and bills to pay. "While it was probably the job I most enjoyed, the down side was the pay. My son was born in 1980, and I had responsibilities. So, I took a job with the local newspaper, in sales." While on the surface, such a change seems quite radical, in many respects, Jerry's work thus far had prepared him quite well. Further, his sociology was still relevant. Just as important, it was another piece of advice from a friend.

According to Jerry, "Another friend contacted me and said that there was this job at the newspaper, and he thought I would be very good at it. The job was selling ads. Selling was not in my thinking at all, and I told him that I've never sold anything before. But he told me, '...well, it's selling, but it's more like what you are doing anyway. You go out and talk to people, you relate to them, you get to know them and their needs. Anyway, the product sells itself when you do this.' So, I guess I let him talk me into it!" What his friend said was that Jerry was basically doing selling right then, whenever he went to a company and convinced them to invest in, and participate in, the CETA program. If that was not sales, then nothing was. "He then told me, if you can do that, then you can do sales. So, I decided to give it a try." For most of the next 22 years, Jerry did just that. "I really saw what I did as less about sales, and more about partnering with clients to get business in their doors. They did not want me to tell them about their product, or about how to run their business. But they did need help in understanding how to reach people who might want to buy. It was really much more of a relationship than just business. Again, my background in sociology, and my adaptability to different kinds of people and situations, made me successful. I saw myself as less a salesman, and more an expert in an area of business that would in turn help their business grow. That's what they wanted, and that's what I delivered. Within my first year, I'd been advanced in pay four times. Perhaps most importantly, I enjoyed it."

While Jerry was successful at what he did, and enjoyed it, he still harbored other dreams. Coming from his CETA days, he understood the concept of adult education. And, interestingly enough, his alma mater developed a program of adult education. At the request of some, Jerry began teaching again, this time in college degree programs, including both adult and traditional students. Over the years, Jerry has taught courses as diverse as marketing, introduction to business, business ethics, organizational behavior, multicultural perspectives, etc. In fact, Jerry's diverse set of experiences, personal and professional, were well suited to teaching. According to Jerry, "As much as I might have been able to help others in my teaching, I have also learned so much. It has stretched and broadened me. For about eleven years now, Jerry has taught, on a part time basis, where he once was a student. Something else was also going on in Jerry's career. The paper where Jerry had worked for years was sold, and his responsibilities were shifted. He was still in sales, but he was no longer responsible for the area in which he had been so successful. It was not a pleasant experience for Jerry, and he began to reconsider his status and station in life. "Actually," according to Jerry, "I knew my days were numbered there. I didn't just want to walk away. In fact, I wanted to demonstrate that I could still do what I had been doing, though in different areas. And I did. It was very gratifying to be able to show to myself, and others, that I still had what it took to do the job. But, it was also time for a change."

That change was building upon what he was now experiencing in the classroom. "I was finding the classroom experience very satisfying at that time. It was almost overwhelming, especially compared to the full-time work I was doing. I was actually looking forward more to my part-time work than I was my full time work. As time went by, my thoughts and feelings began to completely change. I found that I spent more and more time figuring out how to serve my students and participate in academia. I decided that when the time and opportunities were right, I would make the switch to full-time teaching. This may have come out of my CETA days. But, I found that I really was committed to helping people make wise decisions in their lives." Not unlike several significant others, throughout the course of his own life, had done for him. He has both taken, and offered, advice, wise counsel. He knows what it is to change course, yet build a career around common themes of adaptability and reading people. Today, Jerry is planning for his first year as a full-time faculty member, at age 55. So, what is he thinking? "I'm just so challenged right now that I'm willing to work as long and as hard as necessary to do this. I just want to be the best instructor there is at this college. That is my true endeavor." There is little doubt that Jerry will do just that.

28.

SOCIOLOGY AND CAREERS
IN VIRTUAL SOCIOLOGY

Anthony Hollister has had a long, productive and varied career, with over 150 works to his credit, including articles, monographs, motion pictures, and patents.   He has taught in an array of universities including Northwestern, Yale, Rutgers, Nebraska, and Colorado. He has served as researcher, consultant, or entrepreneur, for the Naval Research Laboratory, The National Learning Center's Capital Children's Museum, the Responsive Environments Foundation, Inc., and Rocky Mountain Inventors and Entrepreneurs Congress. In the fifty years since his graduation from a small college in Nebraska, one characteristic can be said to highlight Anthony's career; cutting edge. It is in this regard that Anthony's latest work has taken him into a realm which might be called "virtual sociology".

From his days as an undergraduate, Anthony has had a complex set of interest which included an interest in both mathematical logic and human behavior. According to Anthony, "I found a way to combine math and sociology in the writings of George Simmel. His formal sociology was appealing and suggested a kind of geometry of the social sciences. Such thinking opened the applications of mathematical logic to the various forms of human interaction, structures, and processes. Actually, the abstract side of my interests developed first, then came applications. But while I liked logic I also had other interests. My roommate was also in sociology and together we were state champion debaters. We even considered becoming lawyers." In three years Anthony completed his undergraduate degree in sociology. Among the deciding factors favoring sociology were, according to Anthony, "...the discipline's 'openness'. There are lots of different avenues for a student in sociology to take. Sociology truly is multi-disciplinary."

Subsequent to graduation Anthony served three years in the military during World War II. Interestingly, Anthony encountered film, to which he would return in his professional career, while earning a diploma from the Air Forces Technical School in photography. After his honorable discharge at the end of the war Anthony enrolled in a master's program in sociology which ultimately led to a Ph.D., also in sociology. While formal sociology was Anthony's real interest, it was his math and logic skills which were immediately in demand. "My first teaching was in math logic. And, when I took the position with the Naval research lab, it was my expertise in math logic which they really wanted." In the years just after earning his Ph.D., Anthony's developing interdisciplinary capabilities were being recognized with a variety of grant and invited research opportunities. It was in this way that Anthony became involved with the Naval Research Laboratory (NRL).

It was at the NRL that Anthony began to work with ideas and problems which began to transcend the traditional boundaries between sociology and technology. As Anthony puts it, "We were really at the forefront of a new field, systems analysis. The task was to create a calculus for human problem solving. My abilities in mathematical logic were well suited to this and served as my primary means of entre to the NRL. As part of the sociometric system section the focus was on small group research. The calculus we were developing for decisions and problem solving was actually a first step in the development of artificial intelligence, the matching of human to machine." As work progressed at the NRL it became evident that sociological perspective was both necessary and productive.

One of the initial NRL projects to which Anthony was assigned was the development of a teaching aid for sailors. According to Anthony, "...NRL brought together a very interesting array of people; people with diverse intellectual and technical abilities. It was a fertile area for ideas. Essentially, we progressed from formal systems to computer technology." A latent function of this work was an invention which combined technology with an innovative understanding of teaching and learning systems. This invention came to be known as the "talking typewriter."

As with much of what Anthony has accomplished, the talking typewriter had a genesis in Simmelian sociology. Based on the concept of play forms and a theory of folk models, Anthony sought a way for children to play and simultaneously learn to read. Through some serendipitous contacts Anthony contracted with the McGraw-Edison Co. which invested $1.3 million to develop the idea into a reality. Five engineers, working eighteen months, eventually made the device. The idea was that as a child explored the talking typewriter he/she would strike a key and the machine responded by saying the letter's name. Keys struck sequentially and constituting a word were also spoken. What made this "play" was that the talking typewriter responded to the child but without instruction. According to Anthony, the results were quite significant, and constituted order-of-magnitude gains in reading. The same principle and device could also be used for learning another language, such as French, and math.

Anthony immediately piloted the talking typewriter among inner city children, including preschoolers. While the results were dramatic, according to Anthony, "I nonetheless ran into the very real problem of social change. My success employing the talking typewriter with disadvantaged children seriously challenged commonly accepted notions of education. Further, my success with the poor and minority really did frighten the elite." Eventually, the resistance was so significant that Anthony quit the project. However, the success of the talking typewriter was just the beginning of Anthony's journey into the melding of sociology and technology.

Careers in Sociology

Subsequent to this experience with the talking typewriter Anthony established, in 1962, the Responsive Environments Foundation, Inc. (REF). According to REF's web page, the foundation "...is a nonprofit, tax-exempt organization incorporated in Connecticut. The purpose of REF is to serve as a catalytic agent in bringing sophisticated interactive technology to the world of education. The special strength of the foundation lies in its ability to quickly assemble outstanding professionals who are willing to serve as "trouble shooters" on perplexing educational problems. The Foundation's own research effort is known as the Clarifying Environments Program (CEP). The thrust of CEP is to design learning environments which produce order-of-magnitude gains in acquiring basic intellectual skills."

Through REP and CEP Anthony continued to challenge conventional wisdom in teaching and learning, always exploring the outer limits of educational technology. Products of his efforts include a voluminous array of articles, monographs, and commentaries which explored topics such as, Autotelic Responsive Environments and Exceptional Children (1963), Technology and Behavior (1964), From Tools to Interactional Machines (1965), and Purpose and Learning Theory (1968). Anthony began to apply for patents for his ideas in educational technology. To date these total 36 claims. And, Anthony also took his ideas into film. He had already produced a three-part 16mm motion picture in 1960 entitled, *Early Reading and Writing*, Part 1: Skills, Part 2: Teaching Methods, and Part 3: Development. In each part young children, in some cases beginning at 2 years and 7 months, are shown "reading a first-grade story, printing the alphabet, and typing (with correct fingering) on the electric typewriter. Documentary footage is presented of the learning of complex skills before the age of three as one phase of a higher-order problem solving and social interaction research program." Anthony returned to film in 1971 with another production entitled, *Black Excellence*. This film begins with the 1969 riots in Pittsburgh and moves to the CEP program of cutting edge methods and technologies, employed among African-American children in Pittsburgh's inner city ghettos. In Anthony's words, the film was "a graphic presentation of educational technology with a human touch-- breaking the barriers of the ghetto." In 1974, through REF, Anthony produced a follow-up to *Black Excellence*, this one entitled *Reaction to Black Excellence*. This sequel demonstrated the reaction to the efforts of the CEP program through 1974. Two themes were emphasized in *Reaction...* One was the "lock-out" by the school, parental protests and the eventual moving of the CEP to another location. The other theme demonstrated the high levels of academic achievement of African-American children enrolled in the program.

Concurrent with these activities, Anthony carried on an active and aggressive academic career. From 1947-1952 Anthony advanced from a graduate student lecturer to an assistant professor of sociology at Washington University in St. Louis, MO; during the 1950-51 academic year

Anthony was on leave from Washington University and served as a Carnegie funded teaching associate at Northwestern University; from 1952-53 Anthony served as an assistant professor of sociology at Tufts University, and while there gained entre at the Naval Research Laboratory (NRL) System Coordination Project; from 1953-54 he worked for NRL as a social science analyst; from 1954-57 Anthony was an assistant professor of sociology at Yale University and subsequently became a full professor of sociology and a fellow of Davenport College from 1957-63; from 1963-65 Anthony served as a professor of sociology at Rutgers; and from 1965-89 Anthony held several positions within the University of Pittsburgh. Currently Anthony is an adjunct professor of sociology at the University of Colorado.

One of the consistent qualities of Anthony's tenure at any of the above institutions has been interdisciplinary scholarship. According to Anthony, "Any single discipline is much too narrow in scope. The particular advantage of sociology is that it is precisely not narrow. If your discipline precludes other points of view then there will be a built-in bias and weakness. Teamwork is the key. We must be able to look across the various fields of inquiry if we are going to make progress. In fact, in my current teaching, I spend a lot of time with engineers."

Today Anthony is as active as ever, and still residing on the cutting edge. The latest REF project is referred to as "A Self-Discovery System" (SDS). Returning to the formal sociology of George Simmel and the concept of the play-forms, Anthony has sought to create virtual systems in which a person can participate in a meaningful social scenario. For example, people in crowds, from fans at an athletic contest to participants in a riot, tend to produce behavioral results which individuals would not normally choose. How does this happen? Actually, it is a very complex phenomenon and participants often cannot even tell just why or how they behaved. In some cases individuals make choices and in others the conduct is either irrational or nonrational. Yet something is at work. Anthony's SDS project combines the technologies of virtual reality with a formal heuristic to be able to "see" or "observe" a person in the context of an event, such as a crowd. "I want a person to be able to sense themselves in the middle of a wide variety of environments. I want them to feel what it is like." The objective is a virtual reality stage or chamber, and Anthony is seeking to produce "a successful beta model by the year 2000." To make this happen Anthony is working with technologies such as augmented-tactile sound transducers, immersive animation and "As-If" virtual reality sequencers. With the heuristic devices it will be possible to design and generate SDS scenarios. But of course, "...only a talented, interdisciplinary team can make it work," To this end, "...we have drawn on outstanding engineers, logicians, mathematicians, psychologists, and social scientists."

Though retired, Anthony cannot help but continue to explore the possibilities of sociology. In some ways he was thoroughly grounded in the traditions of the discipline; i.e., Simmel. Yet he was always pushing at the margins, and sometimes producing more resistance than anything else. For this reason Anthony speculates that, "My contributions have yet to make any impact on sociology. Actually, I've had more of an impact on engineers and engineering." Nonetheless, he pursues a "virtual sociology" through his self-discovery system project. "What is evident," according to Anthony, "is that sociology is a *fulcrum for understanding*. It is a point of departure, unlike other disciplines, in that it can bring so much to the table." Not only does the sociologist study human relationships, but the sociologist understands the value of those relationships. Perhaps this is best understood in one of Anthony's other more recent projects, his membership, since 1995, in the Rocky Mountain Inventors and Entrepreneurs Congress. Within this organization are 200 inventors of various interests, ages, and abilities. The purpose is to help those inventors/entrepreneurs along as they seek to develop and protect their ideas. And this is done by bringing together all kinds of experience and expertise. This is the potential of a new *fulcrum for understanding*; a *virtual sociology* creating the conditions for turning dreams into reality.

NOTE:

For more information important to this career, see the following chapters in *Sociology: A Down to Earth Approach,* by James M. Henslin:

Chapter 5   How Sociologists Do Research
Chapter 10 Social Class in American Society
Chapter 12 Inequalities of Race and Ethnicity
Chapter 17 Education: Transferring Knowledge and Skills
Chapter 21 Collective Behavior and Social Movements
Chapter 22 Social Change, Technology and the Environment

25.

COMMENCEMENT,
NOT CONCLUSION

Step #4: "Now That I've Read This Book, What Do I Do Next?"

I do not refer to this section as a conclusion - because that generates an image of being done. The fact is, you have only just begun. This is the same reasoning behind calling your college graduation exercises Commencement. You are beginning! So, in what ways can you begin? Let's start by noting three common elements among the CP's.

First, the CP's evidenced an increasingly common development in modern careers: they are characterized by change. If you do not expect change in your work life then you will most certainly be left "holding the short end" when it comes to career development. In fact, the idea of a career developing implies change. The difference now is that the changes to be expected are generally more radical than in the past. Look back at the CP's and you will see frequent career turns and shifts. These occur within and across job categories. This means both advancement within a job type and organization, as well as movement from one type of work to another. Besides job changes, CP subjects are primed for life changes. The fact is, our lives are made complicated by the presence of others. Because of this we can expect circumstances, especially our relations to others, to be always in some state of flux. As some CP subjects suggested, ten years ago the issues were not AIDS, sexual harassment, diversity in the work place, a world turned upside-down by the collapse of the Soviet Union, an aging population, Enron or 9/11, etc. The sociologist, because of his/her ability to see the "big picture" is in a favorable position to see, or anticipate these trends in their early stages.

A second common element among CP's is a commitment to education and continued learning. In fact, the CP's evidence great diversity, and therefore breadth of perspective, in degrees earned. Bachelor level degrees were earned in fields such as biology, education, nuclear engineering and physics, history, chemistry, and business, as well as sociology. Advanced degrees were earned in fields such as law, criminal justice, business, and communications. Beside, formal degrees, many CP subjects have taken advantage of seminars and professional associations in order to stay on top of their professions. The point is, sociology is a discipline which promotes continuation of the learning process, both in perspective and practice.

The third element in common is what I call opportunism. Because sociologists combine both an anticipation of change with an orientation and an ability to learn, then opportunism is produced. For many of us, an opportunity is something which simply happens. However, an appropriate orientation can produce opportunities. There are three important steps to producing opportunities. These are, 1) actively looking for opportunities, 2) recognizing opportunities when they appear, and 3) taking advantage of opportunities once they are recognized. For example, networking is one way in which opportunities are produced. We all have networks but the question is whether the network is actively operated. If you understand the concept you can employ it, if not then opportunities are limited.

As case in point a current student, Tim, is using sociology as a springboard into international sports management. There are no traditional degrees or career paths for this field. It is possible to dissect the profession and learn its parts, but how does one develop and advance a career. As a part of his studies Tim is engaged in an internship with a major sports event, the annual U.S. Olympic Festival. It is one of Tim's assignments to meet and keep a record of as many Festival organizers and managers as possible. To further his opportunities Tim has printed "business" cards to hand out to those with whom he comes in contact. After the Festival Tim will follow up those contacts with letters. The idea is to begin constructing Tim's network, and his position within that network, as a person who is capable in sports management. In this case, Tim's future will consist of opportunities produced, not just those randomly occurring.

The three elements in common among the CP's, understanding change, pursuing education, and being opportunistic, are only part of the story. Other characteristics possessed by those with successful careers include personal traits such as perseverance and a willingness to work hard. As one CP subject was once advised by his boss, "By themselves little things don't mean a lot, but taken together they mean everything." So, how do you take care of the "little things?" How do you present yourself? How do you speak? What kind of writing skills do you have? Are you capable on the computer? Do you speak a second language? Are you on time? Do you have a reputation for trustworthiness? Do you produce quality work? On this last trait most CP's were of the opinion that ultimately it matters little to those who will employ you just what your degree is. It matters most whether you can "deliver" the work.

The reason for reviewing these characteristics is to emphasize that your career is the result of a set of conscious choices and actions. The better your insights and information about the circumstances you are in, the better your choices and subsequent actions will serve your interests. But this is likely only when you begin the process of taking responsibility for your own future. If you recall, in Chapter One I told you about a parent who was concerned about the career prospects of their son's $60,000 college education. The problem is, dollars invested and career development do not smoothly correlate; that is, one does not automatically translate into the other. You must put yourself in a position where you can exercise opportunism. But how is this done?

My advice is to begin acting like a sociologist <u>now</u>, while your options are most available. This is advisable regardless of your major or career interests. One way of doing this is to use the CP's as models for your own research. By this I mean, investigate the careers of those who have gone before you. In my department we frequently bring alumni and current students together so that students can explore for themselves life after school. Alumni can easily draw connections between courseware, such as research methods, and their careers.

Alumni also serve as excellent first steps in networking. However, not all departments are set up or are capable of accessing alumni. This does not mean, however, that you must get along without this critical resource. A fairly brief on-line search reveals literally hundreds of sociology associations, societies, committees, departments, etc. Three of special note are:

Society for Applied Sociology
http://www.appliedsoc.org/

Sociological Practice Association
http://www.socpractice.org/

American Sociological Association, Section on Sociological Practice
http://www.asanet.org/sections/socpractice.html

Through associations like these, and others, you can begin to gain access to rosters of sociologists representing a wide variety of career paths and specialties. My recommendation is that you simply make contact with organizations such as these, and seek to meet those whose careers have already been launched. You will be surprised at just how helpful, and friendly, professionals in the field can be. But you will not know this for sure unless you make the first effort.

In addition, actually go through the workbook in the appendix of this book. "A Workbook for Job Seekers in Sociology" is an essential and practical guide to the early steps of career development. Here you will be confronted with the necessary choices inherent in designing your career path. Remember, the acquisition of any particular job, and in turn the development of a career, does not just happen. By taking on the challenges presented you will be practicing now the skills you will need for the next forty to fifty years!

Step #5: The Objective is Relevance

Now I will conclude. It has not been my intent to talk you into making sociology your academic major or your career. I do believe, however, that sociology can significantly enhance any career you choose.

Therefore, I do recommend you take this course and this book seriously. But more than this, take what you learn from the classroom and from this book to your life outside the classroom. Be aggressive about it. Ask questions. See what others who have gone before you have experienced. Ask your professor to bring alumni to class. Check into the various sociology websites and begin researching the careers of other sociologists. Ask the questions you have written in the margins. Challenge the common assumptions. Expect change. Learn about your world. Be opportunistic. Your future is not a simple statistical function of chance. It is a function of conscious choice and intentional action. Therefore, look for the opportunities, see the opportunities, and seize the opportunities.

Ultimately the objective is relevance. You want yourself, your life, your work and career to be meaningful, to make a difference. The CP's modeled this in a variety of ways. And that is the beauty of the discipline. It can be relevant regardless of the circumstance. However, you must be prepared, you must be responsible, you must articulate some values around which your future can be focused. Mere activity is meaningless. A job for a job's sake will not take you far. But through this course, and perhaps with the help of this small book, you have begun a process of consciously choosing and producing a life characterized by relevance and meaning. I have often said that there is no life story that I do not see as an unfolding adventure. I look forward to the unfolding of yours.

BIBLIOGRAPHY

Henslin, James M. *Sociology: A Down to Earth Approach*, Second Edition. Allyn and Bacon, 1995.

Howery, Carla. "Teaching High School Sociology." ASA Footnotes 13, no.4 (1984).

"Sociology Series GS-184." Position Classification Standard, U.S. Office of Personnel Management (Office of Classification), December 1988.

Stephens, W. Richard (Jr.). "What Now? The Relevance of Sociology to Your Life and Career." From, Using Sociology, Second Edition, Roger A. Straus, Editor. General Hall, Inc., 1994.

APPENDIX

The following materials constitute a practical guide to job acquisition and career development. This "Workbook" is a special contribution to Careers in Sociology by the Society for Applied Sociology. The authors are Catherine Mobley, Ph.D., Clemson University, Stephen F. Steele, Ph.D., Anne Arundel Community College, and Kathy Rowell, Ph.D., Sinclair Community College. Together, Drs. Mobley, Steele, and Rowell have created a meaningful template for you to begin considerations regarding your future.

A Workbook for Job Seekers in Sociology

Drs. Mobley, Steele and Rowell provided the original version of this workbook as part of popular presentations at the annual SAS conferences. The authors of this booklet generously donated the copyright to the Society for Applied Sociology. The organization is exceptionally grateful for their loyal support. Our thanks go out to these authors:

Catherine Mobley, Ph.D., Clemson University

Stephen F. Steele, Ph.D., Anne Arundel Community College

Kathy Rowell, Ph.D., Sinclair Community College

Layout and editing by Teri Kepner, Administrative Assistant, Society for Applied Sociology.

TABLE OF CONTENTS

Step 1: Why Do You Need This Booklet?

First, for this booklet to be successful, you need to identify your career direction.

What are your reasons for using this booklet?

Please check all of the following which apply to you:

What is your highest degree in sociology?

- ❑ Less than a Bachelors
- ❑ A Bachelors
- ❑ A Masters
- ❑ A.B.D.
- ❑ Ph.D.

- ❑ I am just starting out with a degree in sociology.

- ❑ I am considering a transition from academia to applied sociology.

- ❑ I am considering a transition from applied sociology to academia.

- ❑ I am just curious about the career opportunities open to sociology majors.

Step 2: Where Have You Been?

It's important to look at where you've been in order to have a clear understanding of where you want to go. Many career handbooks advise job seekers to take the time to develop a work-leisure autobiography. This exercise is invaluable for forging ahead in your job search in applied sociology.

Be as thorough as possible in writing your personal autobiography. Here are some questions to get you started:

Why did you originally decide to major in sociology?

In your educational experience, which courses have you liked the most? (You can include both high school and college courses.)

While in school (or even out of school) have you written any papers or produced any documents that you are particularly proud of? If so, list their titles below.

What guidance have you had about careers in sociology?

Step 3: Where Are You Now?

Now it's time to conduct a real-time personal inventory regarding your skills, personal attributes, etc. so you can have a better sense of where you CAN and WANT to go in the future.

Please write your answer to the following questions:

What are your strongest personal skills or characteristics?

What are your strongest "sociological" skills and abilities?

What are your personal weaknesses?

What are your "sociological" skill and/or ability weaknesses?

What additional skills do you feel you need to be successful in today's job market?

Step 4: Where Do You Want to Go?

Now, take a moment to write a personal vision statement. Briefly, where do you want to go? Of course, we're thinking about a career here, but you can't envision a career without a view of other important elements in life; family, leisure, community involvement, etc. We've presented this vision statement in three "chunks of time": next year, three years from now and ten years from now. Please write about your future as you see it in those three time frames.

Next year I hope to:

In three years I hope to:

In ten years I hope to:

What Do I Do Next?

Put steps 1 through 4 together:

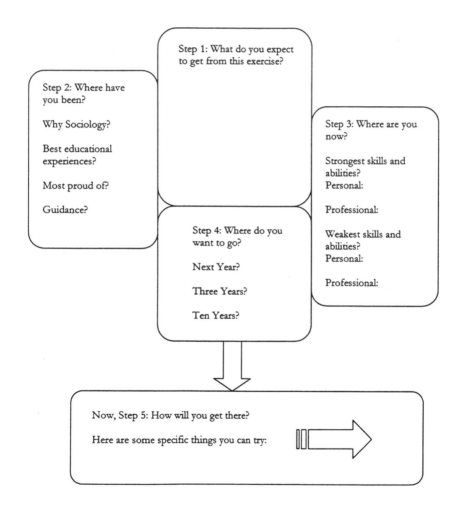

Step 1: What do you expect to get from this exercise?

Step 2: Where have you been?

Why Sociology?

Best educational experiences?

Most proud of?

Guidance?

Step 3: Where are you now?

Strongest skills and abilities?
Personal:

Professional:

Weakest skills and abilities?
Personal:

Professional:

Step 4: Where do you want to go?

Next Year?

Three Years?

Ten Years?

Now, Step 5: How will you get there?

Here are some specific things you can try:

Step 5: How Will You Get There?

In this booklet we'll look at five strategies for "hunting down" a job and, hence, reaching your future vision. Taking these in turn, we'll review:

> Networking
>
> Informational Interviewing
>
> Mentoring
>
> Interning
>
> Volunteering

For each one, we'll define the strategy, why you should do it, when it should be done, and then, perhaps more importantly, address HOW you can do it. Let's GO!

Strategy 1:   Networking

Thoughts to Consider
Be Positive, Proactive and Plausible. Network among yourselves and with professionals and professional organizations that can lead you where you want to go.

WHAT IS IT?

Networking is the process of developing and nurturing your direct and indirect social ties and career contacts to create your own career and help others build their careers.

WHY DO IT?

To beat the system

Make yourself a "known quantity"

For advice and ideas

For leads and referrals

For moral support

Other reasons?

WHEN TO BEGIN?

➤ The sooner the better.

➤ It takes time to develop and nurture contacts.

➤ Don't stop once you find a job. Networking is a life-long process!

➤ Think about the internal networking you need to do within your organization.

➤ Effective networking can mean the difference between a successful career and a lackluster career.

➤ Network among your peers as well. They can be a good source of information.

➤ You may want to consider drawing a "network map" to gain a better idea of how to achieve your career goals.

NETWORKING: HOW TO DO IT

Use as many "channels" as you can to reach your envisioned career target. Here are some examples:

➤ Word-of-mouth. Ask about jobs that might be available, and listen for opportunities.

➤ Letters. These work, but they may quickly get "trashed" or worse yet "filed forever!" Better to follow up a letter with a telephone call or a personal appointment.

➤ Friends and acquaintances. Very likely, someone, somewhere who is directly or indirectly associated with you is "connected" to a job or a person who is near the job you want to have. Ask your friends and make new friends. Widen your network sphere.

➤ E-mail and the Internet. Get on appropriate listservs and expand your personal e-mail connections.

➤ Professional organizations. Think about making an investment to join a professional organization that caters to individuals with career objectives similar to your own. Don't just join. Get involved!

Thoughts to Consider
We must make a "plausible argument" that sociology is valuable.

NETWORKING: LET'S DO IT!

What is your target job or career?

WHO WILL YOU INCLUDE IN YOUR NETWORK?

Now, make lists of all the people who can help you or who might know about this job or career.

Provide name, telephone number, email address and the date you plan to call your contact.

Friends	Telephone Number	Email Address	Date you will contact

Family Members	Telephone Number	Email Address	Date you will contact

Colleagues	Telephone Number	Email Address	Date you will contact

Acquaintances	Telephone Number	Email Address	Date you will contact

Strangers	Telephone Number	Email Address	Date you will contact

Notables in the Field	Telephone Number	Email Address	Date you will contact

Additional tips:

➤ Benefits aren't immediate: networks aren't built in a day.

➤ Avoid "crisis networking": calling on people when you are in desperate need for employment and/or career advice.

➤ Always report back to anyone that gives you a lead.

➤ Include a wide variety of people in your network; "cast your net wide", so you can draw on people with varied strengths and interests.

➤ Be sympathetic and helpful to those who attempt to network with you in the future.

➤ Don't expect instant answers or results: Think of networking as gardening. You are planting the seeds for future benefits!

Notes:

Thoughts to Consider

Let's stop talking to ourselves. Sociology for sociologists is a losing proposition. Better odds: Sociology for society: Business, Health Care, Government, Education etc.

Don't wait for the "Wanted: Sociologist" ad. Expand your job search to other categories.

A Sociology degree is not an end in itself. Extend your skills and tools.

WHAT IS IT?

A practical application of networking.

Face-to-face meeting with knowledgeable people to gain first-hand information about an occupation.

WHY DO IT?

To obtain high quality information

Explore different career options

Enlarge your network

Get your foot in the door

INFORMATIONAL INTERVIEWING: HOW TO DO IT?

Use your network list from step 1 above to identify a "key informant" you feel could possibly put you in touch with others who are "in the know."

Conduct basic research about the person and the company.

Conduct the interview!

Background research on the company:

Name of company/organization:

Company/organization size?   Years in operation?

What does this company/organization do?

How could a sociologist potentially contribute to this company's or organization's goals?

Background research on the individual you will be interviewing:

Name:

Phone/Fax: Title:

Date/Place/Time of meeting:

Who is this person and what does she/he do? Is she/he the right person?

How do I know about this person?

What do I hope to gain from this meeting?

Additional tips:

> ➢ The golden rule of informational interviewing: never ask for a job! Do not confuse the situation.

> ➢ Don't worry about imposing on the individual. In most cases, they will be impressed (and flattered) by your request and your motivation.

> ➢ Be sure to send a "thank you" note to the individual you've interviewed, telling them how much you appreciated their time, what you learned from the interview, and how you plan to follow up.

LET THE INTERVIEW BEGIN!

Treat like a normal interview, **except** you have a little more "control" in this type of interview.

Questions to consider:

How did you get started/interested in the field?

What steps did you take to get where you are now?

What entry-level jobs are best for learning as much as possible about this field?

What is the typical career path for advancement based on performance?

_____

_____

Some additional questions:

How important is further education in your field for career advancement?

What do you like most about your job?

What do you like least about your job?

If you could start all over again today in launching your career, what steps would you take?

Who else should I talk to about my interests?

Person #1:
Name:

Phone:

Title:

Comments (relation to the individual; field of expertise; place of employment, etc.):

Person #2:
Name:

Phone:

Title:

Comments (relation to the individual; field of expertise; place of employment, etc.):

Important! You may be tempted, but do not ask for a job; ask for information only.

Asking for a job may damage your credibility and confuse matters. Even if offered on the spot, say you would like to think it over first. Don't forget to write a thank-you note!

Strategy 3:   Mentoring

Thoughts to Consider

Start your sociological socialization earlier. Don't wait until graduation. Start today, but encourage the earliest possible start in thinking about a sociology career.

Find a mentor. Search for and associate with someone in the field (or in other fields) who has the character and skills you admire or want to acquire and who is doing the work you want to do.

WHAT IS IT?

Usually refers to relationships between two individuals, usually of different ranking, for express purposes of enhancing the career potential of the junior and perhaps, the status of the mentor.

WHY DO IT?

Critical source of career development.

A source of coaching, a way to "learn the ropes."

Enlarge your network.

Protection: a buffer of support in times of trouble.

Exposure: Creates opportunities for you to succeed.

Benefit to mentors: They contribute to another person's development; gain research
support from the protégé, and learn new perspectives from their juniors.

Additional tips:

A mentoring relationship takes time and initiative to develop and maintain.

Be sensitive to the changing needs that arise in a mentoring relationship.

When it's time to let go, let go. This is actually a sign of growth and achievement.

MENTORING: HOW TO DO IT?

Become familiar with the mentoring culture within your department or organization. Does the culture nurture mentoring or is it fraught with competitive pressures?

Start with professors at school.

Start with co-workers, supervisors.

Investigate whether any professional associations have student-mentoring programs.

Don't rely on one mentor. One person cannot fulfill all your professional needs.

MENTORING: LET'S DO IT!

Who is available for mentoring inside your department or organization?

Identify "department heroes"; people you "want to be like."

Who is (are) this (these) person (s) and what does she/he do? Is she/he the right person?

Name:

Phone/Fax: Title:

Date/Place/Time of meeting:

Name:

Phone/Fax: Title:

Date/Place/Time of meeting:

Identify what you want and need from the relationship: what can you offer?

How will this change over time? Both of you must gain from this to be successful.

What characteristics and skills does this person have that you would like to have?

What opportunities is this person likely to make available to you?

What can you bring to the mentoring relationship?

Who is available for mentoring outside your academic department/organization?

☐ Friends and colleagues that you admire.

☐ Peers: Develop the idea and practice of peer mentoring: how can you help each other to succeed as applied sociologists?

☐ Professional organizations. The Society for Applied Sociology has a mentoring program!

Identify people you admire and "want to be like."

Who is (are) this (these) person (s) and what does she/he do? Is she/he the right person?

Name:

Phone/Fax: Title:

Date/Place/Time of meeting:

Name:

Phone/Fax: Title:

Date/Place/Time of meeting:

Identify what you want and need from the relationship: what can you offer?

How will it change over time? Both of you must gain from this to be successful.

What characteristics does this person have that you would like to have?

What opportunities is this person likely to make available to you?

What can you bring to the relationship?

Strategy 4:	Interning

Thoughts to Consider

Develop and translate skills in addition to research (group process, planning, TQM, evaluation, etc.)

Develop your methods and statistics skills. Don't just "get through" these. Learn and apply them well.

Theory really is important, but it must be conveyed in a practical and understandable way.

Enhance creativity and critical thinking. Be able to conceptualize and solve problems.

Develop oral and written communication skills.

Develop skills outside sociology. Courses and experiences in business, government, health care, computer science, etc. Speak their language.

WHAT IS IT?

➤ Work related experiences which allow you to learn more about a job and career

➤ Unique form of work experience: there is a common understanding between employer and intern that the internship is a source of learning about a particular field.

WHY DO IT?

➤ Provides exceptional career exploration opportunities

➤ A way to gain direct work experience

➤ Enlarge your network

➤ Get your foot in the door

➤ Experience the relationship between theory and practice in a non-threatening way.

➤ Benefit to employer: An internship is a "low-cost" way for your employer to evaluate you as a potential employee

---

INTERNING: HOW TO DO IT?

Identify what you want and need from an internship.

What do you want to learn?

      " When I finish this internship, I want to know/gain experience in the following."

1)

2)

3)

What skills do you want to develop/utilize?

"When I finish this internship, I want to be able to do the following."

1)

2)

3)

What specific tasks would you **not** want to do?

"If I take on this internship, I would prefer not to have to do the following:"

1)

2)

3)

Do you absolutely need a paid internship? If, "YES," this may limit your possibilities. Then,

➢ Conduct research into available internships. The library has many resources about internship possibilities, as does the internet.

➢ Explore more formalized internship programs through your department or through professional associations.

➢ See the following page for additional ways to create internships!

Notes:

There are no limits to internship possibilities! Be creative!

Think about ways in which you can create your own internship opportunities:

I can create an internship in the following ways:

1) Networking with:

2) Information interviews with:

3) Through my mentor, in the following ways:

4) Additional ways (library research, WWW sites, etc.):

The process of looking for an internship is similar to the traditional job search. Treat it just as professionally.

Thoughts to Consider

Ask yourself why you chose sociology in the first place.

Proactively deliver your research and practice to the community (campus and local) in which you reside. Public relations is needed. Get your findings in the local paper. Get local and national recognition.

Embed your research work in the community, make your work indispensable to important community groups.

WHAT IS IT?

An unpaid position, usually with a non profit, that provides an opportunity to get involved with local issues and to meet individuals that could be possible mentors and sources of contacts for paid employment.

WHY DO IT?

➢ An opportunity to help others: intrinsic value

➢ Flexibility

➢ A respected way to gain experience and contacts

➢ Provides exceptional career exploration opportunities

➢ Enlarge your network

➢ Get your foot in the door

➢ Relieve stress associated with the job search

➢ A way to obtain references

➢ Benefit to volunteer organization

VOLUNTEERING: HOW TO DO IT?

Think of the following:

1)   I would like to volunteer with the following groups of people:

I would like to volunteer on the following social issues:

Contact the local volunteer bureau (state and local) to find out what organizations are in need of volunteers.

Organization:

Phone/Fax: Contact:

Organization:

Phone/Fax: Contact:

Organization:

Phone/Fax: Contact:

Make an effort to go in for a face-to-face interview to arrange for your volunteer placement (rather than arranging it over the phone). Identify a person in charge:

Who is (are) this (these) person (s) and what does she/he do? Is she/he the right person?

Name:

Phone/Fax: Title:

Date/Place/Time of meeting:

The local newspaper often lists volunteer opportunities. Be VERY clear about what you want to do and the amount of time you are able to commit.

" When I finish volunteering, I want to know/ do the following."

1)

2)

3)

"As a part of this volunteer experience, I would rather not participate in the following."

1)

2)

3)

Please be aware of the following before you volunteer:

➢ It is easy to over commit to a volunteer organization because the needs are so great. Be sure you can follow through on your commitment.

➢ A volunteer position should be treated with the same respect and professionalism as paid employment.

Thoughts to Consider

The majority of career resources suggest that over 50% of jobs are currently posted in cyberspace. As of 1995, 50% of large and medium organizations used the web to track electronic resumes.

WHAT IS IT?

The World Wide Web is a system of internet servers that support specifically formatted documents. The documents are specially formatted documents. The documents are formatted in a language called HTML (Hyper Text Markup Language) that supports links to other documents as well as graphics, audio and video files. This means you can jump from one document to another by simply clicking hot spots. There are several applications called Web browsers that make it easy to access the web.

WHY DO IT?

➤ It is a quick and inexpensive way to look for jobs and internships.

➤ Geographical distance is no longer an issue. The web is a great place to search for jobs and internships for those living in smaller communities and network areas.

➤ Women and minorities will find many career sites that are useful to them.

➤ Non-profit and governmental jobs are easily located on the web.

➤ It is a great tool for networking.

WHEN TO BEGIN?

It is never too late or too early to start searching the web for possible careers and internships. However, to seriously start job hunting on the web, you will need to develop an electronic resume. There are several new books on the market concerning the writing of an electronic resume (see bibliography). A recent article by Rebecca Smith highlights some of the key factors in writing an electronic resume in a July 1996 article entitled "Byte-able Resumes: Resumes that Computers Can Sink Their Electronic Teeth Into" (Computer Bits Magazine). This article is available on the web as well (www.eresumes.com). Once you have an electronic resume, you are ready to start a serious search on the web.

HOW TO DO IT?

All of the previous steps discussed in this workbook can be easily applied to the web. The key to job searching on the net is patience. There are many resources available on the net concerning careers and internships. Some of the information is free but many of the electronic resume services do have a cost associated with them. However, it would be advantageous to connect with an on-line job finder and resume writer if this is something you can afford. Last but not least, we would suggest that you seek out a web site created by Steve Lodin at Purdue University. Steve has been working in the area of electronic job searching since long before the web became a reality. He has created a web site that discusses how to find a job on the web. This site contains a listing of almost every electronic career resource on the web. This is by far the most comprehensive listing on the web. Connect to:

www.cs.purdue.edu/homes/swlodin/article.html

or

www.cs.purdue.edu/homes/swlodin/jobs.html

for more information. We have also included a listing of several of the top rated sites for job searching on the web at the end of this workbook.

Thoughts to Consider

In the world of cyberspace, the web has enabled many people to create their own jobs and businesses. There are several new books out on the market concerning the use of the web to create new jobs. The opportunities are unlimited!

List below the web sites that you have searched and found useful in electronic job searching. Also, remember to use your bookmarks when searching the net, to save sites that you find useful.

Site Address:	Cost?	Type of jobs?

Please note that web sites change often. It is a good idea to make a hard copy record of any information you find helpful to your job search.

Step 6: What Else Can You Do?

Thought to Consider
"Sociologist heal thyself!"

How do you keep track of all this information and record your job search experience?

ORGANIZATION is important! Develop an applied sociology portfolio! Keep records/files of your job search, both successes and challenges. Possible items to include:

➢ Classified ads/job descriptions
➢ A calendar marking conferences, interviews, seminars, etc. that are pertinent to your job search
➢ Cover letters/rejection letters
➢ Notes/reflections on interviews
➢ Recommendation letters: general and specific letters
➢ Phone numbers, fax numbers, e-mail addresses of contacts
➢ Copies of school documents: transcripts, writing samples, list of courses

Make sure these items are all up-to-date!

What should you do once you find a job?

Continue nurturing your contacts and broadening your networks. Help others to apply the same strategies that proved successful for you:

➢ Be an active part of someone else's network!
➢ Offer to be the subject of an information interview!
➢ Volunteer to be a mentor!
➢ Create internship opportunities in your organization!
➢ Create volunteer opportunities in your organization and get involved in your local community!

How can you continue to be successful?

Apply the five career strategies in many different ways. Use all or one; make it a part of a conscious job search strategy! **PEOPLE are your greatest resource!**

Step 7: How Can You Learn More?

We've put together a bibliography and some information about World Wide Web sites, both of which may be useful for your continuing job search and career building process.

> *Career Resources Bibliography*

Career Information

Altman, Don. 1996. <u>Digital Frontier Job and Opportunity Finder: Tomorrow's Opportunities Today</u>. Los Angeles: Moon Lake Media.

Eikleberry, Carol. 1995. <u>The Career Guide for Creative and Unconventional People.</u> Berkeley: Ten Speed Press.

Everett, Melissa. 1995. <u>Making A Living while Making a Difference: A Guide to Creating Careers with a Conscience</u>. New York: Bantam Books.

Frothingham, Andrew. 1996. <u>How to Make Use of a Useless Degree: Finding Your Place in the Postmodern Economy</u>. New York: Berkeley Books.

Gerberg, Robert Jameson. 1993. <u>An Easier Way to Change Jobs: The Complete Princeton/Masters Job Changing System.</u> Englewood, Colorado: Princeton/Masters Press.

Johnston, Susan M. 1995. <u>The Career Adventure: Your Guide to Personal Assessment, Career Exploration, and Decision Making</u>. Scottsdale, AZ: Gorsuch, Scarisbrick.

Lathrop, Richard. 1996. <u>Who's Hiring Who?: How to Find that Job Fast.</u> Berkeley: Ten Speed Press.

Lauber, Daniel. 1992. "Nonprofit Job Finder." Riverfront, Illinois: Planning Communication Press. A state by state guide to locating non-profits and the job market in each state. A good source of information.

O'Brien, Jack. 1993. Kiplinger's Career Starter: Your Game Plan for a Successful Job Search. Washington, D.C.: Kiplinger Books.

Petras, Kathyrn and Ross. 1996. JOBS 96. New York: Simon and Schuster. This book is published yearly and is a very good job source book.

Richardson, Bradley G. 1995. Jobsmarts for Twentysomethings. New York: Vintage Books.

The Wall Street Journal publishes several good books on Networking, Resume Writing and Interviewing.

Woodruff, Cheryl and Greg Ptacek. 1992. 150 Best Companies for Liberal Arts Graduates; Where to Get Winning Job in Tough Times. New York: John Wiley and Sons. This book is an excellent resource for generating ideas for jobs. One does not need to limit a job search to these 150 companies, but rather gives a broad, general overview of the types of jobs a liberal arts graduate could do.

Internship Ideas

Smith, Cotrell (ed.). 1990. Great Careers: The Fourth of the July Guide to Careers, Internships and Volunteer Opportunities in the Non-Profit Sector. Garret Park, MD: Garrett Park Press.

Resumes

Career Press (ed.). Resumes! Resumes! Resumes! 1995. Hawthorne, NJ: Career Press.

Corbin, Bill. 1993. The Edge Resume and Job Search Strategy. Carmel, IN: UN Communications.

Faux, Marian. 1995. The Complete Resume Guide. 5th edition. New York: MacMillan Press.

Hansen, Katherine. 1995. <u>Dynamic Cover Letters: How to Sell Yourself to an Employer by Writing A Letter That Will Get Your Resume Read, Get You an Interview, and Get You the Job!</u> Berkeley: Ten Speed Press, 1995.

Kennedy, Joyce Lain and Thomas Moore. 1995. <u>Electronic Resume Revolution</u>. 2nd. ed. New York: Wiley and Sons. (This is an excellent resource).

Tepper, Ron. 1992. <u>Power Resumes</u>. New York: Wiley Press.

Other note: There are numerous books on resume writing and job searching. Many are tailored to specific careers. When writing a resume to a specific type of position, it is a good idea to check to see if there are books available on applying for a job in the specific field.

There are numerous resources available on the Internet and World Wide Web. Take advantage of this tool as you create your career in sociology! Also, be aware that web addresses, web information, etc. changes on a daily basis. Be creative and find some additional sites to help you as you attempt to get a head start on your career in applied sociology.

The Monster Board: http://www.monster.com

This career site features job opportunities from around the country and beyond. This site is a fee-based service but charges are directed toward the employer. Job seekers can send them a resume, search through job listings and even review profiles of the company.

ON-LINE Career Center: http://www.occc.com/occ/

One of the internet's longest standing career resources. OCC is sponsored by a non-profit association of leading corporations.

E-Span Career Site: http://www.espan.com

This site features Resume Pro and Career Pro Data Bases.

Career City: http://www.Careercity.com

This site provides more information on issues like resumes, cover letters, interviews, dress, how to explore the hidden job market, conferencing and general job searching. It is a useful place to understand the electronic job search.

Careers and Jobs: http://www.starthere.com/jobs/

This is one of the most complete job databases on the Internet. Its unique feature is hundreds of job listings and connections to other career-related sites. You can also find information about job fairs and resume development services.

Adams JobBank Online: http:/www.adamsonline.com

This website, which is maintained by Adams Media Corporation, provides leads to jobs in technical, computer and medical fields. However, with a little creativity, there are also some links to some sociological careers. Job-fair listings are also posted at this site.

America's Job Site: http://www.ajb.dni.us

This comprehensive site contains information concerning over 250,000 jobs. The list is compiled from other lists provided by the over 1,800 state employment services around the country.

Boldface Jobs: http:/www.boldfacejobs.com

Not only does this website provide information about thousands of jobs, but it also allows you to become even more active in your job search: think about posting your resume in their database!

Career Mosaic: http:/www.careermosaic.com

Another list of thousands of jobs, this site also provides some helpful information about the job search itself. Another unique feature of this web-site is its link to companies that are currently hiring.

Career Path: http:/www.careerpath.com

This comprehensive site provides you with classified ads from major newspapers around the country, including: *The New York Times, The Washington Post, the Chicago Tribune, the Boston Globe, and the Los Angeles Times.*

Notes, Doodles and Deep Thoughts

Give us your feedback!

We hope you enjoyed working through the *"Workbook for Job Seekers in Sociology."* We are interested in receiving your feedback about the workbook as we are striving to improve the resources for job seekers in sociology.

1) What did you like most about the workbook?

2) How could the workbook be improved?

3) Did you apply any of the steps outlined in the workbook? If so, please describe and give us some feedback about the successes and challenges you faced.

4) Any other comments?

Your name_____Date:_____

Address:_____
—

City, State, Zip_____

E-mail address:_____

Thank you for taking the time to complete this form. Please mail it to this address in the enclosed business reply envelope:

Society for Applied Sociology
Division of Social Sciences
Anne Arundel Community College
101 College Parkway
Arnold, MD 21012

_____

_____

NOTES

NOTES

NOTES